Our culture typically trivializes names—and people. Elizabeth Mulloy shows another way, a way in which naming and new-naming dignifies and deepens human beings. Her crisp and alive writing shows how it happened among our ancestors, and how it can continue to happen among us. This wonderfully written exposition lays clear the substrata of names and naming that are so richly foundational in the Scriptures and makes them accessible for contemporary faith.

Eugene H. Peterson

In her first book, Elizabeth Mulloy brings fresh insight to ancient truths. Far from being another know-yourself-in-order-to-feel-fulfilled kind of book, *Your Secret Name* deals with *true* identity and how becoming the persons God created us to be enables us to honor the Creator Himself.

There is good balance here. Ego is seen as important but it's kept slim, healthy but not puffed up. The focus is clearly on Jesus Christ and the mystery of His life within every believer.

Elizabeth Mulloy, ever the teacher, has written a book for every Christian who is eager to learn and grow, as well as for those who enjoy reading a well-written book. I commend *Your Secret Name* to you, for I believe it will be both profit and pleasure to your soul.

Colleen Townsend Evans

ELIZABETH MULLOY

Your Secret Name

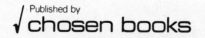

Published by
chosen books

FLEMING H. REVELL COMPANY
OLD TAPPAN, NEW JERSEY

Library of Congress Cataloging-in-Publication Data

Mulloy, Elizabeth.
  Your secret name.

  "Chosen books."
  1. Identification (Religion) 2. Christian life—
1960–   . 3. Mulloy, Elizabeth. I. Title.
BV4509.5 1988   233   87-32219
ISBN 0-8007-9124-X

A Chosen Book
Copyright © 1987 by Elizabeth Mulloy
Chosen Books are published by
Fleming H. Revell Company
Old Tappan, New Jersey
Printed in the United States of America

To Mother and Daddy,
who prayed us
into the Kingdom

Like many Kingdom efforts, this book represents the skills, resources, and prayers of many brothers and sisters. I owe so much to them for their faithful help, that I can only hope I've said proper "thank you's" along the way and that the Lord will reward them richly. Most especially, I thank my husband, Michael, and our daughters, Meg and Kit, for their loving encouragement.

CONTENTS

FOREWORD

"Be . . . all that you can be!" challenges the U. S. Army recruitment ad. "To thine own self be true," advises Polonius in Shakespeare's *Hamlet* (and each spring untold commencement speakers echo his counsel). "Tap your inner consciousness and develop your full potential," invite the Rosicrucians in a back-of-the-magazine come-on. Beer merchants flatter their potential market: "You're on your way to the top, and on the way *you know just who you are!*"

The world calls to us from every direction. From pulpits to fitness studios, the pitch is on: Find yourself! Know yourself! Love yourself! Assert yourself! Maximize, actualize, realize yourself!

While some reject the question "Who am I?" as sophomoric and self-indulgent in a world where children are starving, others answer the call gladly and devise widely diverse and ingenious means to achieve the ultimate goal of self-fulfillment.

Some are lucky enough to have a definite gift, such as musical talent or athletic ability or physical beauty, which shapes their identities from childhood on. Others, unaware of any outstanding traits, "find" themselves by aping the current look or political stance or moral posture of world figures with strong identities, lapsing into caricatures of a Brooke Shields, a Gloria Steinem, a JFK. Still others, wanting to be unique, rebel against the prevailing fashion or morality, seemingly unconscious that their rejection of one culture has simply catapulted them into a counterculture with its own expectations and pressures to conform.

Some of us define ourselves (and others) by work (I'm a computer programmer; I'm "just" a housewife), by race (He's a black lawyer), by religion (I'm a cradle-roll Methodist; he's a dyed-in-the-wool Catholic), by education (He's a Harvard man, you know) or a cause (He's a Marxist; she's one of those "women's libbers"). Others, weary of the search, borrow their identities, letting themselves be defined by relationships (I'm Joe's wife, Karen's husband, Tom and Kathy's mother). We look for our identities in our roots, in our stars, in our biorhythms, in the approving faces of others.

And most of us find answers—for a time. External identities, invented selves, suffice for a season. But even if we do get it all together and, wonder of wonders, "find" ourselves, we learn that our satisfaction is tenuous. Sooner or later dreaded beasts like Mid-Life Crisis slouch in, hissing, "Is that all there is?" Or retirement or a spouse's death or the empty-nest syndrome knocks down the scaffolding of our identities and we suffer a profound and frightening loss. Who am I *now*? we fret, now that my work (my family, my looks, my talent, my strength . . . and people's expectations), the things that once defined "me," are gone?

Or, now that I am finally free to express myself . . . who am I supposed to express? F. Scott Fitzgerald wrote of his personal identity crisis: "It was strange to have no self—to be like a little boy left alone in a big house, who knew that he now could do anything he wanted to do but found there was nothing that he wanted to do."

The passionate search for a "name," for our true identities, for the fulfillment of our personal destinies is not the exclusive quest of twentieth-century America or even of the "me" decade. "Who am I?" is perhaps the most ancient of all questions. And like a chronic itch, it will not go away. The good news is that there *is* an answer for each one of us, a true, eternal, and individual answer. We have merely forgotten where to look for it.

I certainly looked for *my* answers in every direction possible. A Southern girl, reared to please others at all costs, I became, for the first part of my life, the product of the "oughts" and "shoulds" of family and hometown. Ironically, when my heart finally rebelled against the blueprint of a life spread out before me, I had been so well-trained that even in rebellion I conformed like a chameleon.

From the respectable expectations of my parents I swung wildly into the new morality and situational ethics of my contemporaries. Drugs, casual sex, the whole lifestyle of the '60s left its mark on me, till I had little sense of personal conviction. Trading pieces of myself away for approval, I covered myself with a patchwork garment of other people's values, all the while yearning for integrity—that quality of being morally and intellectually consistent, complete, and whole.

At twenty-seven, frustrated in marriage and career, I found myself returning to the religion of my childhood, long since abandoned in my quest for individuality. To my surprise I found that the Jesus Christ I had once loved as a literary character was a real and living Personality with whom I could have a personal relationship. I gave my life to Him.

According to the Bible I had become a new creature. And truly, I felt new motives, new joy, and certainly a new peace in my heart. But some old habits were still operating. All my life I had been taught to approach people and situations defensively—learning to take on the talk, the dress, the thinking, the lifestyle of those around me—a kind of protective coloration, as it were. Now I am a "Christian," my mind told me, I will have to figure out how a "Christian" looks, thinks, and acts.

The irony of my task was great. Before I had entered the Kingdom of God, I had viewed Christians as a monolithic collection of clones—toothy, not too bright, smiling sweetly as they packed for the next boat to Africa or China. I had always feared that to become a Christian was to lose what little identity I had fashioned for myself and be plunged into a grinning sea of anonymous uniformity.

As I began to observe those around me, to read and listen to testimonies, I discovered instead a wide range of people "from every tribe and nation," so various that their only discernible common characteristic was their relationship to Jesus Christ. Yes, there were a few apple-cheeked gospel singers, but there were also intellectuals like C. S. Lewis, writers like G. K. Chesterton, Malcolm Muggeridge, Thomas Merton, poets like Gerard Manley Hopkins and T. S. Eliot, servants like Corrie ten Boom and Mother Teresa, saints from the backwoods like Kathryn Kuhlman, believers from the upper middle class like Charles Colson, pilots and athletes, *Vogue* models and rock stars. The "communion of saints" was far richer than I had ever dreamed.

So accustomed was I to assembling my persona that, as I looked around at the rich diversity of lifestyles within the Christian community, I was confused. "Lord," I asked, "who shall I be? From whom shall I draw my direction, at whom shall I look as role model?"

Getting no answer, I continued to imitate those around me, making tuna casseroles and serving on committees at church, playing the Compleat Charismatic at the prayer meeting, and studying the Bible in an evangelical mode. But no "role" felt totally right and I became frustrated with role-playing. The integrity I had once hoped for still eluded me, and I was about to resign myself to never "fitting" into the Kingdom of God. Perhaps my own feelings and promptings were what I was supposed to "die" to. . . . I didn't realize that I was asking all the wrong questions.

Then one day as I was reading the Gospel of John, the Lord finally broke through to me. John 21:18 tells of Jesus' prophetic description to Peter about his future martyrdom. Peter turns around and spying John, not surprisingly, asks the Lord, "Well, what about him? Is his fate going to be as hard to bear as mine?" But the Lord refuses to compare the two. "If I want John to live until I return, what's that to you, Peter?" He challenges. *"Follow thou me."*

Suddenly I realized that God's plan for me could only be discovered if I, like Peter, followed only Him, not someone else, not even the best Christians I could see around me. He, and He alone, was the "way"; there was no "way" outside of His particular direction to me. And if I ever hoped to find out who I was and what my purpose on this earth was going to be, it could be found in one way only: following Him, answering to Him. If I followed the One who had created me, the One who alone knew me far better than I knew myself, there was no fear of being cloned or of becoming a lifeless stereotype. And best of all, I didn't have to produce an identity or a life's work. That would be *His* gift to *me!*

As the years have passed—nearly fifteen now—I have seen this come to pass. It is not yet easy to keep my eyes on Him alone; it is never too easy to obey when He points me upstream or calls for me to differ from other believers around me. But I know that His way is the way to life, and that it will be the Lord alone to whom I am accountable for those gifts and opportunities He has entrusted to me.

As I have seen others struggling with the question of identity, their purpose and their destiny in life, my heart has yearned to share the answer I have found—even more so to those in the Kingdom who have not yet discovered their uniqueness to God and their place in His redemptive work.

It is for these people that I have written this book. It is my prayer that they will believe and receive God's wonderful promise to them:

And you shall be called by a new name *which the mouth of the Lord will give.*   Isaiah 62:2

1

THE GIFT
OF IDENTITY

What's in a name? In an era and culture in which people often name their children solely for the purpose of alliteration or because of a name's current popularity, we may think, "Very little." But to ancient peoples a name was a sacred thing.

To previous generations a person's name signified and revealed his or her essence (what the Romans called *quidditas*—that person's "whatness"). A person's name was the key to his or her true identity; it expressed character, position, authority, and function. And in some mysterious prophetic way, it even influenced personal destiny. This belief was so pervasive among Jews that a rabbi once declared: "The sentence of heaven can be diverted by a change of name."

This practice has scriptural backing as the Bible is rich with examples of names that reveal the character of their bearers. Caleb, the elderly Israelite whose name means "all heart," proved it by requesting the most mountainous part of the land of Canaan—leaving more appealing areas for others—when offered his choice by God. Nabal, the surly farmer who by his total lack of hospitality provoked the anger of King David, was as his wife said, a man of his name: "fool." Isaac, whose name means "laughter," was named by God as a reminder to his aged parents of their incredulity at the promise of his birth. Moses, "to draw out," was named for his watery origin in the Nile by Pharaoh's daughter who unwittingly foreshadowed his role in leading his people out of bondage and into covenant with God. And the ultimate fulfillment of Bible names came in the person of Jesus—"God will save"—who was also called Emmanuel, "God with us."

The act of naming was regarded as the most solemn of undertakings, requiring time and thought. Jews named their children on the eighth day, for boys the day of circumcision. Other cultures delayed even longer, seeking wisdom from their gods about such an important matter. Many cultures bestowed private as well as public names, secret names, known only to family, for knowledge of the name gave power and was not to be revealed to strangers or enemies. In still other civilizations, among them the American Indians, young people entering puberty took on new names, names they had sought for themselves in times of fasting and introspection. Even today in Christian cultures young people often take on saints' names at the time of religious confirmation, implicitly, if not overtly, seeking to take on some of the characteristics of the admired forebear.

Throughout Scripture one of the ways God reveals Himself to human beings is as the One who knows their names, indeed, as the One who has given them their names in the first place, even if they themselves are not aware of His existence. In Isaiah 43:1, He bases His righteous claim on the Israelites by virtue of His position as their Father, their

Creator: "I have called you by name, you are mine." In Isaiah 45:3–4, He promises treasures that will prove His presence:

> *That you may know that it is I, the Lord, the God of Israel, who call you by your name. For the sake of my servant Jacob, and Israel my chosen, I call you by your name, I surname you, though you do not know me.*

To the city Jerusalem, which functions as a symbol for all God's people, He explicitly promises a series of names: "In those days . . . Jerusalem will dwell securely. And this is the name by which it will be called: 'The Lord is our righteousness' " (Jeremiah 33:16); "The name of the city henceforth shall be, The Lord is there" (Ezekiel 48:35); "Jerusalem shall be called the faithful city, and the mountain of the Lord of hosts, the holy mountain" (Zechariah 8:3).

When Jerusalem goes through periods of shame, God, who is Re-Creator, Redeemer, and Vindicator, promises to remove her reproach by giving her a new name:

> *The nations shall see your vindication, and all the kings your glory; and you shall be called by a new name which the mouth of the Lord will give. You shall be a crown of beauty in the hand of the Lord, and a royal diadem in the hand of your God. You shall no more be termed Forsaken, and your land shall no more be termed Desolate; but you shall be called My delight is in her, and your land Married.*
>
> Isaiah 62:2–4

When, therefore, God promises His people a new name, He is not merely referring to a different appellation. What He will give them is a new character, a new authority, a new destiny.

In the Old Testament God establishes His place as name-giver to the historical nation of Israel; in the New Testament, He widens the promise to include the spiritual Israel, the future and eternal nation of believers that will span "all tribes and kindred." John conveys this promise to the Church from the Lord Jesus Christ:

*To him who conquers I will give some of the hidden manna, and I
will give him a white stone, with a new name written on the stone
which no one knows except him who receives it."*

Revelation 2:17

These promises have a mysterious intimacy—the revelation not only of new names, but private individual names—
names known only to each person and to God. What is this
secret name of ours that only our Creator knows and that we
can learn only from Him?

As we seek our true God-designed identities, we find a rich
source of insight into both the gift and the giving of it in the
stories of five persons: Abraham and Sarah, Jacob, Simon
Peter, and the apostle Paul. In each of these stories, God
gives new names and then calls forth the character to match
the name He designed. Though He deals in a unique way
with each distinct personality, we will find principles
throughout that will be instructive.

ABRAHAM AND SARAH

To understand the full significance of the story of Abraham
and Sarah we must look first at the story of the Tower of
Babel that precedes it. Mankind, acting without reference to
God, decided to assemble its own resources, build for itself a
city, construct a tower that would penetrate the heavens, and
thereby "make a name for ourselves" (Genesis 11:4). These
aspirations and the fact that they had one language symbolize
their united separation from God, a legacy from Adam and
Eve's rebellion. God in His "severe mercy" decided to stop
their plans before they destroyed themselves in pride, so He
confused their language and scattered them across the land.

A nation *will* be built, but not upon the arrogant designs of
a committee. The nation God desires will be founded upon
the faith and obedience of a man and his wife.

The person God chose to call was a 75-year-old man named
Abram, whose family had come originally from a region

known as Ur of the Chaldees, a prosperous and sophisticated civilization. He was a very wealthy man, owning many cattle and much silver and gold. He was also a man searching for truth; tradition says that his father, Terah, was a manufacturer of idols, but that Abram rejected these on the logical grounds that anything made by the hands of man could hardly possess greater power than the man.[1]

The one thing Abram did not possess was children; his wife, Sarai, was barren and past childbearing age. The supreme irony of his life was that his name meant "exalted father." Sarai's is more understandable: Hers meant "grumbler." Surely this problem was a source of both sadness and bitterness to the aging couple.

It is God who made Himself known first to Abram. Scripture records simply that "the Lord said," and *what* He said reveals Him as a Covenant Maker:

> *"Go from your country and your kindred and your father's house to the land that I will show you. And I will make of you a great nation, and I will bless you, and make your name great, so that you will be a blessing. I will bless those who bless you, and him who curses you I will curse; and by you all the families of the earth shall bless themselves."* Genesis 12:1–3

We can only imagine the awesomeness of this personal revelation to a man who, like ourselves, had been brought up in a materialistic world with little interest in and little knowledge of spiritual truths. Suddenly God, a God Abram had never known, was speaking to the depths of his heart, calling for his response, and promising that if he would believe and obey the Voice, an utterly new existence would open to him.

In an act of faith so radical that it could only have been fueled by God's grace, Abram obeyed, leaving his country and his family—in short, his old identity—and heading for a land he had never seen before. Sure enough, in Canaan God met him again and renewed His original promises:

"Lift up your eyes, and look from the place where you are, northward and southward and eastward and westward; for all the land which you see I will give to you and to your descendants for ever. I will make your descendants as the dust of the earth; so that if one can count the dust of the earth, your descendants also can be counted. Arise, walk through the length and the breadth of the land, for I will give it to you."   Genesis 13:14–17

Without even knowing it, Abram was moving toward a new name. As he "walked the land" he began to experience testing. An earlier sojourn in Egypt, where he had lied to protect Sarai from the advances of the Pharaoh, showed him his need for a deeper reliance on the God who called him. This time, in Canaan, when he battled and conquered an alliance of hostile kings, he gave the credit and praise to God. God's responding revelation of Himself acknowledged Abram's growth: "Fear not, Abram, I am your shield; your reward shall be very great" (Genesis 15:1). Abram, remembering the promise of descendants, cries out, "Where are the children You have promised?" to which God responds by promising a son. He even directs Abram to go outside his tent and lift his face to the billions of stars in the desert sky: "So shall your descendants be." Abram's belief of this promise, as impossible as it seemed, confirmed to God that this man was indeed the one through whom He could rebuild humanity. God, therefore, "reckoned it to him as righteousness." He then renewed and revealed in a vision more of His plan for the age to come.

But the years passed and no child came to Abram and Sarai. Surely their faith was growing as they recited God's words, reminded night after night of His staggering promise of multitudes of descendants. Unfortunately, the independent Adamic nature again asserted itself, and Abram and Sarai tried to fulfill God's promise in a human, logical way, exclusive of God's intervention. God had not yet said whether the son would be by Sarai, so she, following a common practice, offered her younger handmaiden, Hagar, in proxy and Abram agreed. This contrived union did produce a son, Ishmael, but he and his descendants proved to be the nemesis of Abram's offspring from then on. Abram and Sarai had yet to learn that what God promises supernaturally, He delivers supernaturally.

Thus, God waited until Abram was ninety-nine years old to make His next revelation. Now, not only had "the way of women" passed from Sarai (as Scripture puts it) but the "way of men" must have also passed from Abram! Yet this was God's chosen time, and He called upon Abram to forsake his own understanding, his own devices, and walk henceforth in full obedience: "Walk before me, and be blameless" (Genesis 17:1). He continued with the great promises to Abram and He did so in terms of his name:

> *"No longer shall your name be Abram, but your name shall be Abraham; for I have made you the father of a multitude of nations. I will make you exceedingly fruitful; and I will make nations of you, and kings shall come forth from you. And I will establish my covenant between me and you and your descendants after you throughout their generations for an everlasting covenant, to be God to you and to your descendants after you. And I will give to you, and to your descendants after you, the land of your sojournings, all the land of Canaan, for an everlasting possession; and I will be their God."*   Genesis 17:5–8

It is most significant, for our study in finding our own identities, to look at the change in tenses in this passage: "you *will* be," "your name *shall* be," and then, "for I *have made* you." God is saying, "You will be these things I've promised because I have already placed within you the potential for becoming them, even a father of multitudes. These are not characteristics or powers that I will impose on you later, or that you yourself must evolve into or produce on your own in order to fulfill My word. . . ." What was *already* in Abram was now, by God's fiat, quickened.

All those years God had been carving out a place in Abram where He could now dwell, infusing the man with His own

Spirit. Before the foundation of the earth itself, God had designed this man to be the father of a nation, but it had to wait for the assent and preparation of the man.

It is scripturally true that as God gives us our new identity and purpose, He is simultaneously at work at another level. Foundational to God's giving of Abram's new name was the revelation of a new name for Himself. Before this time, God had said, "I am your shield: you don't have to be afraid and tell lies; I am your great reward: you don't have to create the fulfillment to My promises." Here in Genesis 17:1, God revealed Himself in His sovereignty over the universe. He said, "I am God Almighty, El Shaddai." Within this name, according to Nathan Stone, is not only the idea of God's omnipotence over all His creatures but also of His maternal mercy toward them. *Shaddai* comes from a root word for both "mountain" and "breast"; it speaks simultaneously of a father's protective strength and the nurturing care of a mother's body. God was saying, in effect, "I am Mother and Father, Creator and Sustainer, Sovereign Lord over all—all you will ever need. When I say to you that you, too, will be a father of nations, you will know that I and I alone am able to make it come to pass. I establish the laws of nature and I overrule them at my discretion."

The result of this theophany was that any skepticism Abram had had about God's ability to do this thing was now erased, and he was able to receive his new identity. Like the moon reflecting the sun, Abram would grow in fullness as God was magnified in his awareness and esteem.

Abram has become Abraham.

Abraham has been called by God, humbled by his own fears and failures, showered with many blessings, and given a new name; he now anticipates a new destiny.

The same promise will be shared by Abram's wife, for Sarai, too, must participate in this miracle by an act of faith. God removed the reproach of Sarai's sad name as well·

"As for Sarai your wife, you shall not call her name Sarai, but Sarah shall be her name. I will bless her, and moreover I will give you a son by her; I will bless her, and she shall be a mother of nations; kings of peoples shall come from her."   Genesis 17:15–16

What a blessing for the barren, unfulfilled grumbler, the bitterly disappointed one—that she should be called, and should *become* "Sarah"—a princess!

Two relationship changes took place after the intervention of God into the lives of Abram and Sarai, and all affect us today. The first has to do with our fallen nature, as lived out in the lives of Adam and Eve. In Abram and Sarai we see the redemption of Adam and Eve. The biological mother and father who forfeited their inheritance, are superseded, as it were, by a new spiritual mother and father, called by God to initiate the lineage that will ultimately usher in the Messiah. In Adam and Eve, the human race received its biological heritage, its fallen nature, but in Abraham and Sarah—and it is important to note that Sarah's status is exalted in the same way Abraham's has been—we are offered a spiritual heritage that we can enter into by faith. The lineage of Abraham is open to volunteers, for the Israel God has in mind is to be a nation of adopted rather than natural-born sons and daughters.

The second relationship change that affects us as Abraham's descendants is this: Sarah is usually remembered as the one who laughed when she heard the promise of a child. But Scripture says that Abraham also "fell on his face" with laughter when he heard it (Genesis 17:17)! God kept them forever after mindful of their initial skepticism and their subsequent delight by instructing them to name their son Isaac (laughter). Do we glimpse here the restoration of the loving camaraderie that may have characterized divine-human relationships in Eden? Has God begun the process of infusing His personality into man's, a healing that will be fulfilled in the Messiah?

According to Michael Esses in *The Phenomenon of Obedience,*

Jewish commentary on this story of the changed names notes that God inserted an "h" into both names and suggests that God took the letter from His own name—the tetragrammaton YHWH, the ineffable name of God that we call Yahweh. Whether true or fanciful, the notion reflects the infusion of God's personality into them both and the reawakening of their ability to enter into a deep relationship with their Creator. The spiritual capacity that had been stunned into dormancy by human rebellion, the sterility of spirit that had passed down through subsequent generations, has been reversed by the intervention of God's own Spirit.

As God brought Abraham and Sarah into the reality of their new names, He showed divine patience. In times of lapsing obedience, such as when Abraham repeated to Abimelech the lie he had told to Pharaoh, God was forbearing. When Sarah was cruel to Hagar and jealously sent her away, God forgave her and provided graciously for the slave woman and her son. God used this patience as He called Abraham and Sarah deeper into His confidence, making Abraham privy to the inner workings of divine justice. When the sin of the cities of Sodom and Gomorrah had outstripped the bounds of even His mercy, God told Abraham of His righteous obligation to destroy such wickedness so that Abraham might pray for the innocent people who lived there, too. We see in this particular story how great and discriminating was God's mercy as He taught Abraham the dynamics of intercession. And day after day, El Shaddai provided for their every need, abundantly, creating within their inmost hearts a muscled, seasoned faith.

Most of all, through the special joys and trials of parenthood, He taught Abraham and Sarah the deep lessons of sacrificial love and utter vulnerability to another human being. Through this greatest of blessings, their son Isaac, God called forth and defined their true identities; through Isaac God thrust them into the white heat of the refiner's fire, to purify the gold of their faith.

We find this story in Genesis 22, a story that strikes a terrible wonder into the heart of a mother or a father. Scripture tells us that God called for the sacrifice of Abraham and Sarah's son of promise. It does not tell us any details of Abraham's agony nor his deliberations; it simply says that on the following day, "Abraham rose early in the morning" (Genesis 22:3). Had the situation ever been put to him hypothetically, surely he would have rejected it as impossible. El Shaddai would never mimic the unspeakable cruelty of the gods of Ur. In reality, God seemed to be calling back from them the most precious gift He had ever given, the constant living manifestation of His power and love. Surely Abraham would never have suspected that within his heart sufficient trust for such a test had been built.

But the writer of Hebrews tells us that Abraham "considered that God was able to raise men even from the dead" (Hebrews 11:19). He had known in his own body, and in Sarah's, God's power to make alive and fruitful that which was quite dead. He gambled now that resurrection was well within the grasp of his friend, Almighty God.

And yet . . . in those awful hours when faith struggled with human experience and empirical reality, back and forth, step by step up Mt. Moriah, Abraham's heart was stretched and molded by fire into conformity with the heart of his Creator. God was giving Abraham a taste of what so many centuries later He would feel as He voluntarily sacrificed His only Son upon this same mountain. How gladly we read the merciful ending of the story, how, just as he would have slain Isaac, Abraham was stopped by an angel of God and directed to a ram caught in the bushes nearby—a sacrifice "provided by God" as Abraham had reassured his frightened son.

A few years after Sarah had been "gathered to her people," in the biblical phrase, Abraham died, too, having lived to a "good old age." In their lives, with all their particular details, we can see a broad pattern for the relationship God carries on with all those who believe.

First, He calls His people by name, one by one, calling them out of the realm of "sight," that dimension limited by human understanding and experience, and into His fuller Kingdom where they have not traveled before. At crucial times, He reveals His own identity to meet their needs. Then, in some way, by direct or gradual revelation, He gives them a glimpse of who they shall be and what purposes they shall serve in that Kingdom. Throughout, He goes about creating their days to bring the Word, the idea of them, into flesh-and-blood reality. As we shall see, at least "the *edges* of His ways" are echoed in the stories that follow.

JACOB TO ISRAEL

The story of Abraham's grandson, Jacob, begins with a prophecy given to his mother before he was born. Though Rebekah and her husband, Isaac, loved each other very much and had been married for many years, they waited a long time for a child. When Rebekah finally became pregnant, she found she was carrying twins, and Scripture says that the children "struggled together within her." She asked God, "If it is thus, why do I live?" and the Lord answered her, "Two nations are in your womb, and two peoples, born of you, shall be divided; the one shall be stronger than the other, the elder shall serve the younger" (Genesis 25:22–23).

Two babies were indeed born, the first so covered with hair that they named him Esau ("rough"). The second was born hanging onto his brother's heel, so he was called Jacob (supplanter, usurper). According to the custom of primogeniture, the elder son, Esau, was destined to inherit the lion's share of his father's lands and possessions.

The prophecy that the elder would serve the younger was, therefore, in contradiction to the normal scheme of things. Rebekah must have pondered this prediction as she experienced their unusual births, along with the ominous statement that they would live in enmity.

As the boys grew it was not difficult to see their differences.

Esau, a hunter, became a man of strong appetites who desired immediate gratification of his physical needs.

Jacob developed into a more homebound man (and was his mother's favorite) tending his father's flocks. Though his will was just as egocentric as his brother's, Jacob wanted the promises of God, the blessing of the prophecy. His heart became fixed on somehow managing to seize his brother's birthright for himself. And in this personality trait, it seems we glimpse something of the mystery of names. That is, God wants to give us blessings; He does not want us to seize them on our own.

But Jacob did not yet know this. One day Esau came home from hunting famished, and Jacob saw his chance. Preying upon his brother's weakness, Jacob offered the stew he was making for a trade—the birthright. Esau, ruled by his belly, agreed. What a clear revelation of the characters of the two men: Jacob, the opportunistic conniver, and Esau, whose contempt for abstract things led him to forfeit his inheritance rather than miss a meal.

What happened next is parallel to Abraham and Sarah's attempts to fulfill God's promise in a human way. When the day came for the aging Isaac to confer the birthright upon Esau, along with a patriarchal blessing, Jacob and his mother did not trust God to intervene. Instead, they conspired to obtain the blessing by their own devices. To disguise Jacob as his hairy brother, Rebekah put the skins of goats on his hands and neck. Then she prepared Isaac's favorite food for Jacob to take to his father as a further enticement.

Their plan succeeded. Isaac, trusting his own failing sight rather than his spiritual discernment, failed to recognize Jacob. He pronounced the blessing, which was irrevocable, on his younger son. Moments later Esau arrived and, to his horror, discovered that all of his inheritance had been given to his brother. Murderous in his rage, Esau vowed to kill Jacob, and Jacob was forced to flee.

And here we encounter a second mystery illustrated in Jacob's story. God wishes us to yearn passionately for His blessings. When He does not find this in us, the Bible uses a strong word "hate"; when He does find this passion in us, the Scripture uses the word "love." Let's see how this unfolds in Jacob's story.

Encountering the narrative of Jacob and Esau in the Bible we feel surprised that the hero of the story turns out to be Jacob, the unscrupulous. We feel sorry for Esau; we sympathize with him, even though he is culpable for his own loss. We may even be more put off by such a passage as Malachi 1:2–3 in which the Lord says, "I have loved Jacob but I have hated Esau." Surely Jacob's methods were not acceptable to a just and righteous God! No. What God "loves," that is, what He can *relate* to in Jacob, is the man's passionate desire for God's blessings. Esau the materialist had, like Adam before him, despised his birthright. God can find no dwelling place in such a heart, no basis for fellowship with such a nature. Jacob, on the other hand, wanted the birthright, even though he resorted to reprehensible means to go after it. With a heart that is willing to seek such things, that desires the fulfillment of God's promises, God can make contact; and those whose methods are corrupt, He can teach how to receive in a godly way, by faith.

In this episode, we get a graphic allegory of a profound spiritual truth: Our first-born nature, carnal like Esau, has no time, no taste for things that are eternal, godly, in the future. In our human nature, we are bound by the law of self-preservation and, thus, live at the beck and call of our physical appetites and our emotional and intellectual desires. It is not until a spiritual nature (the second-born) has been given from God that we have the capacity to raise our sights above purely earthly aspirations and satisfactions.

Even though his deeds were despicable, Jacob had this capacity, so God could walk with him. In his years of exile, the conniver would encounter—and not by accident—just the right circumstances to turn him into a man of God.

Rebekah helped her son once again, arranging for him to go to live with her brother Laban in Haran. After a journey of forty miles, Jacob lay down in the wilderness to sleep, and dreamt of a ladder reaching from earth to heaven, filled with angels of God ascending and descending. In the dream, the Lord revealed Himself as the God of Abraham and Isaac, and He renewed the terms of the covenant He had made with them, adding a promise to Jacob to accompany and protect him wherever he went. Jacob awoke astonished and fearful. "Surely the Lord is in this place; and I did not know it. . . . How awesome is this place! This is none other than the house of God, and this is the gate of heaven" (Genesis 28:16–17). In response to this revelation, Jacob built an altar and promised a tithe to God of all that He will provide.

In this episode, we see a sinful man's first encounter with a holy God. Jacob had spent his life thus far in a home where God had been talked about; surely he was steeped in the stories of his grandfather Abraham and the mighty miracle of the birth of his own father, Isaac. Yet, until this night, he had had no contact of his own with Almighty God, no personal knowledge of El Shaddai. Now, to his chagrin, he recognized that there was no gulf between heaven and earth: God had been there all the time, seeing his deeds, weighing his heart.

All his life, Jacob had lived solely for his own advancement, regardless of the means. Now God had shown him that his actions were not hidden from the courts of heaven. The smoldering wick of conscience, an awareness of his sin was being fanned into tiny flame.

God followed this revelation with a series of sore trials and great blessings—typical of the way He works with us in preparing us for our new name. These trials and blessings *both* would shape Jacob into a fit vessel for God's grand purposes.

Arriving in Haran, Jacob went to work for his uncle Laban, who offered him wages for his labor. Jacob had by this time fallen in love with Laban's younger daughter, Rachel, and he agreed to work for Laban seven years for her hand in marriage. Scripture notes that those seven years "seemed to him but a few days because of the love he had for her"

(Genesis 29:20). Like Abraham and Sarah's wait for Isaac, these years must have stretched Jacob's capacity to honor a commitment, besides heightening his capacity to love another person above himself. This period must also have taught him the satisfaction of working hard and honestly for something, rather than attaining it through guile.

Jacob also learned how it feels to be fooled. On his wedding night, he discovered that Laban had given him not Rachel but Leah, her older, "weak-eyed" sister. Laban coolly rationalized the switch: "In our country, we *never* give the younger before the elder. . . ." Perhaps Jacob's own words of self-justification came back to haunt him: "But after all, God did promise that *I* should have the birthright." Laban did give him Rachel, too, but on the condition that Jacob work an additional seven years.

As gracious compensation during the following years, God then poured out the blessing of many children upon Jacob and his two wives and two concubines. Eleven sons and one daughter filled his tents, the sons destined, along with Benjamin, the twelfth son who would be born several years later, to head the twelve tribes of the nation of Israel. Likewise, Jacob's flocks flourished in strength and number because of the supernatural wisdom given him by God, whom Jacob freely credited for his success. Laban naturally wanted Jacob to stay with him forever to increase his own flocks, but relations between them were deteriorating, and God told Jacob it was time to go back home.

On the way, Jacob received the distressing news that his brother Esau was coming to meet him with four hundred men. To save at least part of his family, Jacob divided them into two companies. But then he did a significant thing: He prayed to God for help. The nature of his prayer shows a heretofore uncharacteristic level of humility and dependence on God to save him:

"O God of my father Abraham and God of my father Isaac . . . I am not worthy of the least of all the steadfast love and all the faithfulness

> *which thou hast shown to thy servant, for with only my staff I crossed this Jordan; and now I have become two companies. Deliver me, I pray thee, from the hand of my brother, from the hand of Esau, for I fear him, lest he come and slay us all."*   Genesis 32:9–11

The old schemer was still at work, however, because Jacob backed up his prayer by arranging for a series of appeasing gifts for Esau to be sent ahead of his caravans. Then he sent his family and flocks across the stream ahead of him.

Jacob was left alone, and *because* he was alone he was at last ready to receive his new identity. Isolated, afraid of his vengeful brother, without wives, family, servants, or herds to distract him, Jacob finally had to face what he had done to Esau and to consider the justice of his brother's wrath. Arthur Pink has observed: "To be left alone with God is the only true way of arriving at a just knowledge of ourselves and our ways. . . . No matter what we may think about ourselves, nor yet what men may think about us, the great question is what does God think about us."[2]

A war had begun in Jacob's heart: Against his old habit of self-justification struggled the dawning conviction of his sin. This inner battle is mirrored in the strange events of that night:

> *. . . And a man wrestled with him until the breaking of the day. When the man saw that he did not prevail against Jacob, he touched the hollow of his thigh; and Jacob's thigh was put out of joint as he wrestled with him. Then he said, "Let me go, for the day is breaking." But Jacob said, "I will not let you go, unless you bless me." And he said to him, "What is your name?" And he said, "Jacob." Then he said, "Your name shall no more be called Jacob, but Israel, for you have striven with God and with men, and have prevailed."*   Genesis 32:24–28

A strange story, and yet what an apt allegory for the struggle between human pride and the righteous demands of a holy God for repentance. The tenacity of such pride, Jacob's in particular, is shown in the fact that the wrestling match lasted all night long. To end it, the angel of God finally had to exert supernatural means and break its mainspring, as it were, by putting Jacob's thigh out of joint. Even crippled, Jacob hung on until the angel had to call for him to let him go. Jacob, recognizing a superior being, would not do so until a blessing was given.

But before God could bless him, Jacob had to take a crucial step. He had to tell his name. God knew his name; this was not a request for information. What God wanted was for Jacob to answer one question: "Who am I? What is my true name?" All those years Jacob had interpreted his own name in the best way: "I am Jacob: clever, shrewd, wily, resourceful, ambitious." God forced him now to acknowledge its real meaning, and to his salvation, Jacob answered honestly: "Schemer, usurper, thief."

"No more," said the Lord. "Your confession is the beginning of your transformation. From now on, you will be 'Israel,' for you have prevailed in your strife with men and with Me." In a sense, Jacob's new name was given as a reward as well as a prophetic word, even as Abraham's naming came at a time when God wished to commend his loyalty. Yet within the name there is a curious ambiguity. The words *isra*, "he strives," and *el*, "God," can also mean "*God* strives."[3] God had prevailed, too, for it was He who pursued Jacob, wrestled his flesh to the ground, and brought him to a place of repentance.

Just as Jacob had refused to let go of his divine adversary, so God had not relented in His fight to transform Jacob. The nature of wrestling is that the level of each opponent's performance is enhanced by the other's strength and skill. Just as the bodies of wrestlers are entwined, so they are in a sense locked together in a common spiritual outcome. In this unique sport we may see a parallel of our own struggles, and appreciate in a new way the loving perseverance of the One who must conquer us in order to set us free.

But the story does not end here:

> *Then Jacob asked him, "Tell me, I pray, your name." But he said,*
> *"Why is it that you ask my name?" And there he blessed him. So*
> *Jacob called the name of the place Peniel, saying, "For I have seen*
> *God face to face, and yet my life is preserved."*
>
> Genesis 32:29–30

When Jacob asked his name, the man replied, in effect, "Why do you have to ask?" He and Jacob both knew that by now Jacob recognized his opponent as a spiritual being, for he had asked for blessing. Sure enough, Jacob was silent. But after he received the blessing, he shook his head in astonishment: To come face to face with God, the Holy One, would normally mean death to a human, as surely as fire would mean destruction to a piece of wood. And yet . . . "I am not dead!" exulted Jacob.

The ironic thing is that a death *had* occurred. Jacob the conniver had received the death sentence; to God he was as good as dead. But the essential Jacob, now called Israel—the true core of Jacob—was alive! He *had* been preserved, brought to new life, born again by God's forgiveness.

Yet another irony is now operative in Israel's life. Scripture gives us a detail that expresses a spiritual truth: "The sun rose upon him as he passed Penuel, limping . . ." (Genesis 32:31). As Israel went on his way, he was marked in body as well as soul with the knowledge of his dependence on God. No longer was he the egocentric, self-reliant man of the old days, walking where he wished, only occasionally aware of his need for God. Now, with every step he took, he would be reminded of the Lordship and mercy of El Shaddai. Limping, he nevertheless had "the sun rising upon him," for as his life continued, his awareness of the living God, of His power and His majesty, would grow.

Jacob, reunited with his family and reconciled at last to Esau, made a new start, cleaning his house of all idols and dedicating himself to God. His new identity as Israel, the patriarch of the new nation of God, had begun. But Jacob's character didn't change overnight; in fact, throughout the rest of the book of Genesis, he is referred to interchangeably as Jacob and Israel. Positionally (that is, in God's sight), he was a new creature; he was now what God always knew he could be. In the realm of time and space, however, he didn't always walk according to his spirituality. (The same is true for the nation of people that was thereafter called by his name.)

In the years that followed, Jacob knew much sorrow: the defilement of his daughter, Dinah, and the subsequent shame of his sons' ruthless vengeance upon her suitor. The loss of his beloved Rachel and his father Isaac. The years of thinking that Joseph, his favorite son, was dead, and finally the seeming loss of Rachel's only other son, Benjamin, his youngest. Surely, only his relationship with God kept him from utter despair in those times. But by God's grace, Jacob ended his life in honor, pronouncing by God's Spirit words of prophecy and blessing upon each of his sons, giving them God's direction and charge for their lives. When at last he had said all the words given him by the Lord, he "breathed his last and was gathered to his people" (Genesis 49:33). Jacob/Israel was mourned not only by his own family but by a great company of people, including the leaders of Egypt.

2

THE GIFT IN
NEW TESTAMENT TIMES

So far we have considered the stories of three wonder-fully human and colorful people, Abraham and Sarah and Israel. All, of course, were Old Testament characters.

SIMON TO PETER

Though its theme is the same, the story of Simon Peter differs from the Old Testament stories in two major ways. First, in the Old Testament, much is unrecorded; there is much we must infer about the growth of each person as God changes his or her name. Secondly, in the stories of Abraham and Israel, God generally spoke to their hearts, remaining invisible except for occasional manifestations in human form.

With Simon Peter, however, we have a multitude of accounts in the Gospels and in the book of Acts, so that we can trace changes almost from day to day. More importantly, in Simon Peter's story, we see God Himself—Jesus—in an ongoing intimate human relationship. ("The Word became flesh and dwelt [literally, "pitched his tent"] among us," records John.) Thus, in Peter's transformation, we have the privilege of witnessing a full spectrum of "close encounters," and can see how God relates to a man and how He changes him.

Simon's relationship to Jesus began with his brother Andrew's triumphant announcement: "We have found the Messiah!" Andrew, a follower of John the Baptist, had witnessed Jesus' revelation as the Lamb of God, the sacrificial offering that would save Israel from death. Centuries of waiting for God's deliverer, bitter years of oppression, had honed their generation's desire for the Savior. We can only imagine Peter's excitement—and apprehension. Could Andrew be right? Would this indeed be the one?

When they came face to face, Scripture simply notes: "Jesus looked at him" (John 1:42). But the Spirit reminds us that these were no ordinary eyes. These eyes were able to look into a man's heart. The young rabbi spoke, saying in effect, "So, you are Simon, son of Jonah? In time you shall be called Cephas, Peter."

Simon, the Greek form of a Hebrew word meaning "sand"[1]; *Jonah*, meaning "dove." The name Simon bar Jonah, then, suggests vacillation, the impermanence of shifting sand, the unpredictability of a bird's flight—an apt name for a man of quick and fluctuating enthusiasms. But Jesus, looking past this man's current identity, prophesied with authority: "You shall be called a rock."

Simon, now and thereafter called Peter, who knew his own impetuosity, his inconsistency, his vacillating loyalties, nevertheless must have been stirred by Jesus' words. F. B. Meyer writes:

"Ah," said Peter to himself, at the close of that interview, "He little realizes how fickle and wayward I am;
now hot with impulse, then cold as the snows of
Lebanon. And yet if He thought me capable of becoming
rock, and evidently He does think so, why should I not,
with His help, resolve to attain and apprehend that for
which I have been apprehended?"[2]

As it turned out, Jesus was not only speaking of Peter's
future character but also to some degree of Peter's commission, his work among the believers Jesus would win in the
days and years to come.

But how did the Lord turn this sand into rock? The Gospels
trace for us a series of events and revelations.

Two of the first recorded events reveal one of Peter's key
traits. In Matthew 4:18–19 Jesus issued the call to Peter and
Andrew to become His disciples. Even though they were
hard at work casting their nets, so great was their assurance
of His truth that they "immediately" left their entire livelihood to go with Him. This capacity to respond quickly and
thoroughly was perhaps one of the most attractive traits
Jesus saw in Simon and would develop and temper in Peter.

In Matthew 14:22–33 Peter's total, passionate obedience is
again evoked. This time Jesus, after preaching to and healing
great crowds of people, wanted some time alone with His
Father. He stayed behind while the disciples launched out
across the Sea of Galilee. In the middle of the night, they saw
what they thought was a ghost walking across the water
toward their boat, and they were understandably terrified.
But Peter believed that he recognized the Lord; "If it's really
You," he cried, "bid me come to You!"

Peter was not some buffoon showing off in front of his
Master and his friends. Here was someone who so appreci-
ated the supernatural power of Jesus that he yearned to walk
in the same dimension as his Lord. God has called for His
people to walk by faith and not by sight; Peter's impulsive

and, at first, successful foray upon the water was a literal fulfillment of God's own desire.

Then, taking his eyes off the Lord, Peter fell into the waves. We may be accustomed to interpreting Jesus' cry "O man of little faith, why did you doubt?" as a rebuke. But Peter *did* begin. His faith, though incomplete at this stage, had thrust him out of the boat; eleven others, cautious, analytical, merely looked on. Is it not possible that Jesus' question was the cry of a parent whose disappointment at the baby's fall is miniscule compared to the pride he feels in those first steps? The passionate trust of this man's heart, when seasoned and stretched, would be a testimony to the irresistible beauty and power of God.

The next time we see Peter (Matthew 16:13–20), he is again headed for deep water, theologically speaking. The crowds were speculating about Jesus' identity; some were saying that He was a reincarnation of Elijah, Jeremiah, or even the recently slain John the Baptist. Jesus' interest was in His *disciples'* thoughts: "Who do *you* say that I am?"

There are in Scripture heart-stopping moments when we feel God Himself flooding a human mind with divine revelation. Here Peter saw: This holy man was not just an anointed prophet, or even a political deliverer. This man, their teacher, was God's one and only Son, born directly of Him in a way no other human being would ever experience. This man who had eaten, slept, and laughed with them was . . . their Creator. Peter cried out: "You are the Christ, the Son of the Living God!"

The enormity of such a thought might have choked a more analytical man into silence. But Peter, quick to action, had voiced a revelation from God, and Jesus rejoiced: "Blessed are you, Simon bar Jonah, for flesh and blood have not revealed this to you, but My Father who is in heaven. You *are* Peter," He continued in almost a reprise of His initial prophecy, "and upon this rock I will build My Church."

Varied and passionate are the divergent interpretations of this passage, Protestants saying "the rock" is the confession of Jesus as Lord, Catholics insisting that the rock is Peter himself. But could it be that Jesus meant both things? "You, Simon, are a normal human being, but you are a rock, too, for you are responding by your will to a truth God has revealed to your heart. It is upon such human beings confessing My Lordship that I will build My Kingdom. Not merely the correct doctrine held in a human mind; certainly not merely one human personality no matter how appealing or fit for service; but that kind of trusting acceptance of divine revelation that has been shown by Peter. Such people making such confessions link heaven and earth; these are the building material for My Church."

The Gospels show us the events of Peter's apprenticeship: the teachings heard and the discussions afterward, the miracles of healing and deliverance he witnessed (some of them, like the raising of Jairus' daughter, private events seen only by himself, James, and John). On the Mount of Transfiguration (Matthew 17:1–8) again these three were entrusted with a foretaste of the risen Lord when He laid aside His humanity for an instant and let His glorious being shine forth. They would greatly need this experiential knowledge in the days of near despair to come.

Perhaps just as edifying were the times of error, when Peter learned that man's ways are not God's ways. Immediately after his confession of Jesus' Lordship, for example, Peter rebuked Jesus for speaking of His coming death. "God forbid, Lord!" he cried. "This shall never happen to you" (Matthew 16:21–23). Jesus, whose human heart was so deeply bound in love to friends, family, and the earth as to make Him vulnerable to the temptation to flee the cross, in turn rebuked His disciple: "Get thee behind me, Satan." It must have been an overwhelming thing for Peter to realize that by acting from his human perspective he could serve devilish purposes.

Most valuable of all were the episodes by which Peter gained self-knowledge. Having been commended for his passionate loyalty to Jesus, Peter had developed a dangerous mentality: a delusion about his power to resist the enemy. As the Lord and the disciples headed for Gethsemane on that sorrowful Passover night (Matthew 26:31), Jesus told them that they would desert Him, quoting the prophet Zechariah (see Zechariah 13:7): "I will strike the shepherd, and the sheep of the flock will be scattered." In Luke's account (Luke 22:31-34), Jesus specifically turned to Peter with a personal warning: "Simon, Simon, behold, Satan demanded to have you [disciples], that he might sift you like wheat, but I have prayed for you [Peter] that your faith may not fail; and when you have turned again, strengthen your brethren." In his pride and love Peter protested: "Lord, I am ready to go with you to prison and to death." But the Lord answered, "I tell you, Peter, the cock will not crow this day, until you three times deny that you even know me."

In the hours that followed, Peter learned the truth of His Lord's words. Taken along to support Jesus as He struggled to embrace His Father's will, Peter, James, and John fell fast asleep. Filled with anger at himself, Peter then tried to defend Jesus by slashing at a guard with his sword, forgetting in one instant of terror all he had learned in three years with the Prince of Peace. And then, as he cowered nearby during Jesus' interrogation, to his horror Jesus' prophecy came true. The words of a young girl—"You were with this Jesus the Galilean"—frighten him into curses of denial. "I don't know Him! " After three such denials the cock crowed and Peter "went out and wept bitterly" (Matthew 26:75).

The news of Jesus' resurrection—what joy it brought to Peter's heart. He was alive! Just as He said! Even death couldn't defeat Him! Jesus' greeting to him and the others as He appeared in their midst—"Peace"—must have been a balm to Peter's sore, ashamed heart. And yet there was still unfinished business. Knowing that the humiliation of his cowardice had been gnawing at Peter, the Lord graciously addressed his need for forgiveness and restoration.

In the twenty-first chapter of his Gospel, John recorded the final interview between Peter and his Master; in it, we see the merciful yet persistent work of God upon this man's image of himself. In His love He could not leave one shred of delusion in Simon's heart—not if he was to become the rock God had designed him to be. Like Jacob, Simon had to see his true identity clearly before the Lord could transform him into Peter. So the pressure was applied:

> *When they had finished breakfast, Jesus said to Simon Peter, "Simon, son of John, do you love me more than these?" He said to him, "Yes, Lord; you know that I love you." He said to him, "Feed my lambs." A second time he said to him, "Simon, son of John, do you love me?" He said to him, "Yes, Lord; you know that I love you." He said to him, "Tend my sheep." He said to him the third time, "Simon, son of John, do you love me?" Peter was grieved because he said to him the third time, "Do you love me?" And he said to him, "Lord, you know everything; you know that I love you." Jesus said to him, "Feed my sheep."*   John 21:15–17

Calling Peter by his old name, the Lord challenged him with his own words uttered so recently, when the old Peter had proudly declared that he would "love to the death." "Do you love Me more than these others do?" Jesus asked, using the word for divine love. Humbled by the memory of his disastrous betrayal of his Lord, Peter answered, "You know that I have affection for You." "If so," Jesus responded, "feed My lambs." Then again, "Do you have divine love for Me?" "You know that I have affection for You." Peter almost pleaded for the Lord to stop. "Tend My sheep," said Jesus. A third time Jesus said (the three questions seem to redeem Peter's three denials) "Do you even have affection for Me?" and Simon, getting the point, lay his heart before the Lord for *Him* to judge what was inside: "Lord, You know everything." No more proud declarations of "love to the death."

Jesus, on the night of the last Passover meal with His disciples, had told them a central truth:

> *"As the branch cannot bear fruit by itself, unless it abides in the vine, neither can you, unless you abide in me. I am the vine, you are the*

branches. He who abides in me, and I in him, he it is that bears much
fruit, for apart from me you can do nothing."   John 15:4–5

"Even though you have walked and talked with and learned
of Me these three years," He declared, "you cannot in your
unaided humanity do even what you most fervently desire."
At Gethsemane, He had comforted the sleeping Peter, James,
and John with another truth: "The spirit is willing, but the
flesh is weak." Now Peter had learned these truths, not in his
head, but in his bones. Without the indwelling spirit of Jesus
Christ, he himself didn't even have sufficient affection to be
loyal to his Lord. The last vestiges of self-reliance, of human
resolve to do something for God, had been stripped lovingly
from Peter, and he was left shivering with self-knowledge.

But what could the Lord be doing? With each answer,
exposing more and more inadequacy, the Lord was giving
Peter a commission! Feed and tend My flock; teach and lead
My people. The words echoed back to Peter: "When you
return, strengthen your brothers. When you have seen your
own total need of Me, then (and only then) are you fit to
minister to My people." Peter realized that this revelation
was also his commission. Empty, now he could be filled and,
in turn, overflow to others.

The Feast of Pentecost some forty days later (Acts 2) is
regarded as the "birthday" of the Church. It is at Pentecost
that the Holy Spirit, the "Promise of the Father," came upon
the waiting disciples, giving them the supernatural power to
praise God in other languages, heretofore unknown to them,
but recognizable to the worldwide pilgrims to Jerusalem
gathered for the holy days. We might also call it Peter's
birthday, for it is here at last that we see the rock emerging
from the sand.

The psalmist spoke of God his rock, his foundation,
protection, and salvation (Psalms 62 and 94 among many
others), and Jesus defined a wise man as one who built his
house upon that rock (Matthew 7:24). Peter no longer tried to
be the rock; he was now living *on* the Rock. In fact, in Peter's

life from Pentecost on, we see a man living now on the Rock
so fully that he himself became rock-like. Embued with the
Holy Spirit, he exhibited the same characteristics and oper-
ated in the same gifts his Teacher had exhibited. Peter was
not yet complete, not perfect, but was moving toward
wholeness, still learning how to trust more and more deeply
in that new life that had been poured into him from on high.

In Acts 2:14–40, Peter addressed the crowd, understanding
even as he spoke the prophetic passage from Joel 2:28–32
about the outpouring of the Holy Spirit upon all flesh, saying
as Jesus did in *His* first sermon, "Today is this Scripture
fulfilled in your hearing." The Word of God was being
opened to Peter's heart by the Holy Spirit dwelling there, by
the author, as it were, so that the writer and the listener had
connected in the secret place of spiritual understanding.

Standing up to preach, Peter found his words brought
such conviction that three thousand people pressed forward,
crying, "What shall we do to be saved?" Peter, in God's
wisdom, had the answer in that same hour, even as Jesus
had promised: "Repent, be baptized, and receive the Holy
Spirit which has been promised anyone who believes in the
Lord Jesus." All that he had studied, everything that had
been given him, was now being quickened to life.

Episode after episode in Luke's book, the Acts of the
Apostles, shows us the blossoming of Peter's new identity.
In Acts 3, Peter and John on their way to worship found a
lame man at the Temple gate. Looking at him with supernatural discernment, Peter recognized saving faith in his heart.
In Jesus' name, he spoke words that imparted full healing to
long-dead muscles. This was not a new experience for the
disciples, but now they were without Jesus' bodily presence.
Now they *were* the Body of Christ, doing the greater works
that Jesus had spoken of because they could be many places
at once. In Acts 4, the very people Peter had feared most he
now challenged: "Whom must we serve, God or you?" He
really didn't care what they might do to him. Ignoring their
warnings, as soon as he was released, he was out preaching

again. In Acts 5, by the discerning power of the Holy Spirit, Peter rebuked two hypocrites who dared to think that they could lie to God. Fully yielded to the Lord, Peter could now combat evil in the righteous anger of God's authority, not as he once did in his old hot-headed, sword-swinging days. In Acts 8, when a sorcerer sought to buy the power of the Holy Spirit, Peter again acted according to God's leading and not his own.

In the ninth chapter, Peter healed a sick man and then raised an old woman from the dead. It is certain that if Peter still had a scintilla of self-reliance or self-righteousness left in him, these events could have been a snare to his pride. But because Peter had been emptied of any notion of his own power outside of the Lord Jesus, God could pour out the power unhindered. There was little risk now that Peter would take the credit to himself.

As a human being, *in* the world if not *of* it, Peter still had some problems, of course—his prejudice against the Gentiles, for example. Yet in Acts 10, Peter was ready for a new revelation of a magnitude surpassed only by the earlier revelation that Jesus was the Christ. Now Jesus called Peter to put all that his Judaism had taught him upon the altar. The exclusivity of his world view (God's promises were for the Jews only) had to be shattered if, through him, the light was to be taken to the nations. When he obeyed the vision and the call to go and preach to a Roman centurion, Peter found that God's purpose of redemption goes far beyond what he had ever imagined. The important thing here is that Peter the absolutist was now teachable, yielded enough even for such radical assignments. He would in turn help others catch God's vision for the world.

So, we have watched Simon bar Jonah, the man of sand, be transformed into Peter the rock. We have watched as even that new immutable rock was changed as Jesus called Peter to a wider view of redemption than he had ever imagined.

Now in one last episode, we see a most telling response. The Lord Jesus had intimated to Peter that he would die a martyr's death; James, the brother of John, had already been killed and Peter was imprisoned, bound between two soldiers. Yet when an angel came to rescue him, Peter had to be awakened (Acts 12:7)! The man who once trembled at being linked with Jesus was now, in the face of execution, able to fall asleep peacefully. The man of extremes—bravado and terror—was now living in heavenly peace, the "shalom" Jesus had promised.

The events of Simon's transformation are numerous. Perhaps what most reveals his new identity, though, is his letters to the young churches. Here is a true shepherd, a man whom God has led through both suffering and glory and who now can lead God's sheep with tenderness, wisdom, and true *agape* love. The call for gentleness, patience, trust, and humility echoes through these exhortations. What wonderful words from a man who once lived by brash oaths and a ready sword! The heart revealed in these writings is a new heart, redeemed and shaped into the true character God had always known was there.

SAUL TO PAUL

For the last of our five transformed lives, we turn to Paul. Paul is of special interest to me because he so clearly illustrates how well Jesus knows us before we know Him; how with each of us He has a plan for a new identity that is *perfectly* suited to our personality; and how our backgrounds and our enthusiasms are never accidental. Alone among the five we have been studying, Paul changed his own name.

Next to the Lord Jesus Himself, the best known person in the New Testament is the apostle Paul. At first a vicious enemy of Christians, he became, humanly speaking, the father of Christ's Church, founding many congregations of believers and shaping doctrine for the entire Church for centuries to come. He wrote more of the Bible than any other single person, a mighty instrument of the Holy Spirit to convey to the Hebrews and to all nations the truths enfolded for centuries in God's Word. For much of our understanding of the Old Testament, we must thank Paul—for his study, his mastery of the Scriptures, and for the physical and emotional hardships he endured. And we must praise God for his transformation, for he was not always so useful.

Paul had the best of both worlds. Born in the great city of Tarsus, capital of Cilicia, he grew up in a cosmopolitan atmosphere. Tarsus was a free city: Though under Roman rule, it was free from having to pay taxes to Rome and it exercised a certain degree of self-government, unlike Palestine. It was a center of trade, the site of a major university, and of a school of Stoic philosophy. Like any big city of that time, it was also the scene of military maneuvers, gladiatorial contests, and slave auctions. Though Jewish, Paul's father had been given Roman citizenship, so Paul was a freeborn Roman citizen, a position guaranteeing many legal and social privileges. This credential would figure prominently in Paul's odyssey.

At one time, he also found great pride in his Jewish heritage. Writing to the Philippian church, he lists his personal credentials:

> *If any other man thinks he has reason for confidence in the flesh, I have more: circumcised on the eighth day, of the people of Israel, of the tribe of Benjamin, a Hebrew born of Hebrews; as to the law a Pharisee, as to zeal a persecutor of the church, as to righteousness under the law blameless.*   Philippians 3:4–6

Phrase by phrase, this describes someone of impeccable standing. Born to Hebrew parents of the tribe of Benjamin (unlike many, a tribe untainted by intermarriage with pagan neighbors during Israel's tempestuous history), Paul was circumcised on the eighth day. That means that he was made a legal member of the covenant as an infant, his parents having fulfilled the letter of the law. His right standing in terms of the ritual and ceremonial law, the intricate system of rule and lifestyle for the Jews, was also unquestioned: He was "blameless." His position on the Law of God is that of a Pharisee. Developed during the period between the Old and the New Testaments, the Pharisee movement (like the Reformation many centuries later) had developed for one reason: to save God's Word from the corrupting influence of mythologies, pagan philosophies, and internal heresies. Paul is basically saying here that he revered the Law.

He also knew it thoroughly. As a rabbinical student, Paul studied with the famous teacher Gamaliel, onetime governor of the Sanhedrin, the governing body of the Jews of Palestine. So brilliant was Gamaliel's thinking and so honorable was his lifestyle that he was known as "the Glory of the Law." Because of Gamaliel, Paul had the best education possible, not only in the Scriptures and the commentary on the Torah but, in addition, Paul would have studied the Greek and Latin classics and the contemporary writers of his day. This superlative education was an accomplishment that would serve him well in his missionary work. Each rabbinical student also learned a trade so that they would not be a burden to their people; Paul learned to make goatskin tents.

In those days, he was called Saul, probably named after the first king of Israel, also a Benjaminite. The Hebrew name *shaul* means "asked for,"[3] and it is appropriate, for King Saul had been asked for by the Israelites. Living in a theocracy where God led them through prophets and judges made them nervous; they wanted a ruler like all the other nations around them. So God gave them the leader they wanted.

Tall, handsome, and yet humble, the young King Saul made a brilliant start, leading his people to victory over their ancient enemy, the Ammonites. But pride crept in, and a deep vein of self-will began to show itself in a series of disobediences. Told by the prophet Samuel to wait for his return before making thanksgiving sacrifices to God for their victory, Saul lost patience over a delay and usurped the prophet's position, offering the sacrifices himself.

In a later battle, God instructed him to wipe out the incorrigible Amalekites, from their king to their livestock. To the Lord, they were a cancerous influence whom He had sworn to erase from the land. Saul, leaning on his own understanding and courting the favor of the people, only partially obeyed. He killed the women and children, but he left the livestock and the king alive. To Samuel's despair, Saul showed no sense of remorse over his direct disobedience. He was more afraid of men than of God.

Later, as the young David began his military career by defeating Goliath and the crowds took him as their new hero, Saul was so consumed by jealousy that he tried repeatedly to murder his loyal champion. He even issued a death warrant against his own son Jonathan in paranoid fear of his friendship with David. Gradually, his heart fell further and further away from God till he was filled with evil spirits. His sad reign ended in the midst of a military defeat as he committed suicide.

It is sadly ironic that Saul's namesake was starting down the same road. "Zealous for the traditions of his fathers," Saul of Tarsus, in his Pharisaism, began to lose the spirit of the Law he worshiped, throwing all of his considerable intelligence, will, and energy into the eradication of heretics—specifically the followers of Jesus of Nazareth. The first time we meet him in Scripture, he is holding the coats of those who are stoning Stephen to death (Acts 7:58).

It seems that this martyrdom did little to satisfy his lust for purging the world of Christians. Instead, the picture of the dying Stephen, rejoicing and praying for the Lord to forgive his killers, seemed to have ignited an additional flame in Saul. Acts 8:3 tells us that he "laid waste the church, and entering house after house, he dragged off men and women and committed them to prison." (According to William Barclay, Luke employs a verb commonly used to describe a wild animal ravaging a vineyard.) As it affected his royal ancestor, so the sight of true godliness spurred the New Testament Saul to more ferocious hatred.

It was in this rage that Saul took to the road to Damascus, duly authorized by the chief priests in Jerusalem to capture

Christians in that city. We read what happened on his journey:

> *Now as he journeyed he approached Damascus, and suddenly a light from heaven flashed about him. And he fell to the ground and heard a voice saying to him, "Saul, Saul, why do you persecute me?" And he said, "Who are you, Lord?" And he said, "I am Jesus, whom you are persecuting; but rise and enter the city, and you will be told what you are to do."*   Acts 9:3–6

A later account adds these words, Jesus' commission to Saul as he lay helpless and blinded on the road:

> *"But rise and stand upon your feet; for I have appeared to you for this purpose, to appoint you to serve and bear witness to the things in which you have seen me and to those in which I will appear to you, delivering you from the people and from the Gentiles—to whom I send you to open their eyes, that they may turn from darkness to light and from the power of Satan to God, that they may receive forgiveness of sins and a place among those who are sanctified by faith in me."*   Acts 26:16–18

In a single event, God revealed Himself, brought the proud Saul into utter helplessness, and began to give him his new name, as it were, by commissioning him. To his undoing, Saul met Jesus of Nazareth, not as a threat to the holy Word of God, but as its fulfillment, its very embodiment! In light "brighter than the midday sun" the glorified Lord had identified Himself as the very one whose followers Saul was murdering. The name He called out was a specific one, Saul of Tarsus. This was no vague indignation against religious officials persecuting the young Church. Jesus was confronting Saul of Tarsus, about whom He knew everything, down to the least pricks of conscience the rabbi was trying so hard to suppress. Seeing that the proud heart had been crushed, He then quickly gave it a glimpse of redemption. Saul was now "appointed to serve, to bear witness," not just to the

Jews but to the Gentiles as well, to convey the fullness of the good news of Jesus Christ to all the world.

I find it difficult to imagine the stunning magnitude of the experience that instantaneously turned around so adamant, so passionate and brilliant a man as Saul. Gentle Jesus? Not always! With Saul there was no gentle leading into a new identity. Saul was thrown to the ground by the pure power of God. Jesus slew the old Saul and put him onto a new path all in one breath.

To accomplish the task of conveying the Gospel, Saul had to be infused with the Spirit of God, and the Lord sent a local disciple to minister to him. Ananias confirmed Saul's commission, quoting the Lord's words, "I will show him how much he must suffer for the sake of my name." Laying his hands upon Saul, Ananias prayed for him to regain his sight and to be filled with the Holy Spirit. Afterward, Saul went immediately to the other disciples in Damascus and to their astonishment began to preach in their synagogues that Jesus was the Messiah.

That zealous start and its consequences (Saul had to flee the angry Jews in Damascus by being let down out of the city wall in a basket!) set the pattern for the rest of his life. Revelations, glory, suffering, more revelations—with each adventure Saul grew more passionately devoted to his Lord, more experientially knowledgeable of His character, and more singlemindedly committed to bringing people out of darkness and into the light of God's saving love for each of them.

Like Peter, Saul began to experience the pure power of God, anointing him to understand the Scriptures in a new and vital way; to see the Messiah clearly foretold and now fulfilled in the life, death, and resurrection of the Lord Jesus Christ; to heal the sick and raise the dead; to deliver those oppressed by demons; and to preach the Word to every tribe and nation he encountered in three major missionary journeys to the known world. Where he traveled, churches sprang to life and the people wept when he had to move on

(Acts 20:37). The sick were healed when even his handkerchief was placed upon them (Acts 19:11–12), and the demons reacted to his presence just as they had when Jesus was among them. He lived in constant communion with the Lord, and one time he told of being taken up into the "third heaven" and shown such glorious things that he could not describe them (2 Corinthians 12:1–4). So great were the miracles God worked through him that in Lystra the people, thinking him a Roman god, tried to worship him (Acts 14:11–14).

Throughout his life, he wrote the truths God showed him, explicating Old Testament passages and proclaiming the plan of salvation: that by Jesus Christ's sacrificial death, we are reconciled to God, if we will but abandon our own feeble "righteousness" and receive God's gracious gift by faith.

But this same message of freedom pouring through Saul ("Woe to me if I do not preach the gospel," he wrote in 1 Corinthians 9:16) was conversely his cross. Constantly the target of slandering Judaizers (those who insisted that in addition to accepting Christ, a person must *also* keep the entire Jewish Law) or angry Romans, who saw in Christianity a growing threat to their Empire, Saul lived a life of unceasing frustration and danger. Forced into justifying himself in the face of charges against him, he wrote to the believers in Corinth (2 Corinthians 11:24–28) of the cost of his ministry, including being beaten, stoned, shipwrecked, hungry, whipped, and in danger from the Jews and the Gentiles. In addition to these, he wrote also of a "thorn in the flesh," a messenger of Satan, permitted to harass him so that he might not grow proud and puffed up by the "abundance of revelations" God granted him (2 Corinthians 12:7).

About midway into his years of service, Saul and his partner Barnabas were called by the Holy Spirit to be formally ordained to minister to Gentiles. According to all human understanding, this is a strange assignment. Saul's rabbinical background seemed tailor-made for work among his own brothers, and he wrote that he had such a burden for his fellow Jews that he would give up his own salvation to save them. But

God's plan was to send them to meet a much wider, universal hunger, so He pointed Saul to the Gentile world of the Mediterranean. In Cypress, their first convert was the Roman proconsul Sergius Paulus (Acts 13:7); it was also here that Saul began to be called by his Roman name Paul.

In that day, nearly all Jews had two names—a private one for use in their community, a Greek counterpart for public use: Cephas in Aramaic, Peter in Greek; Joshua, Jesus. In Paul's case, being a Roman citizen, he had always had a Roman name. But till now, it must be supposed that he had not used it regularly. Many suggestions have been offered as to the reason.

Early Church fathers like Jerome thought he may have taken it to commemorate Sergius' conversion, as a Roman general often assumed the name of a place he had conquered.[4] Others have surmised that he took it on as a fortuitous aid to his missionary work among the Gentiles. If so, as William Barclay points out, it was a sign that Paul had fully accepted the mission God gave him, "the mark that from this time he was launched on the career for which the Holy Spirit had marked him out and that there was no turning back."[5]

If this is the case, we may also interpret it as the full yieldedness of Paul to all the new identity that God had placed before him. The interesting thing about the name *Paul* is that it means "little." Evidence shows that Paul was a man of short stature, but it is difficult to think, as St. Augustine did, that this referred only to his physical appearance.[6] Could it not be argued that Saul's assumption of this name was the sign of his embracing the deep truth he expressed so often in his writing: that it is in the weak, the humble, the broken—the "little"— that God's power is complete?

Here is a man who had lost everything the world counts as precious: family, home, religion, status as a scholar and a leader of his people, the worldly productivity of middle age, and the deserved peace of old age. And what did he say of that? In the J. B. Phillips translation, we read:

> *I look upon everything as loss compared with the overwhelming gain of knowing Christ Jesus my Lord. For His sake I did in fact suffer the loss of everything, but I considered it mere garbage compared with being able to win Christ.*   Philippians 3:7–8

The end result of God's work in Paul's life was a total transformation. The murderer was now a lover of such passion that he counted every worldly prize as a piece of garbage compared to the pleasure of knowing his Lord. The freeborn Roman citizen had made himself a bond slave (a freed slave who remains in service voluntarily out of love for his master):

> *For though I am free from all men, I have made myself a slave to all, that I might win the more. . . . I have become all things to all men, that I might by all means save some.*   1 Corinthians 9:19, 22

Paul had changed his own name as an outward sign of the inner reality of his life—the paradox he lived in, indeed, gloried in: "I will all the more gladly boast of my weaknesses, that the power of Christ may rest upon me . . . for when I am weak [literally, "helpless"], then I am strong [literally, "dynamite"] (2 Corinthians 12:9–10). As he neared the end of his life (it is believed he was executed in Rome around 65 A.D.), he wrote to his beloved protegé Timothy, seeing in his own transformation the higher purposes of God for all His people:

> *The saying is sure and worthy of full acceptance, that Christ Jesus came into the world to save sinners. And I am the foremost of sinners, but I received mercy for this reason, that in me, as the foremost, Jesus Christ might display his perfect patience for an example to those who were to believe in him for eternal life.*
> 1 Timothy 1:15–16

COMMON DENOMINATORS: THE PATTERN OF GOD'S WAYS

In these five lives, as diverse and rich as they were, we can see some general patterns, some common denominators, in the way God deals with His people.

1. First of all, God revealed some part of His own name to each of these people: to Abraham and Sarah, He was El Shaddai, the covenant-maker; to Jacob, He was the covenant-renewer, the God of Jacob's fathers. To Peter, He was first Jesus of Nazareth, and then the Son of the Living God. To Paul, He was the risen and glorified Lord Jesus Christ. All were called to look upon and recognize His Lordship so that they might trust in what He was going to call them to be and to do. So too, we must learn who He is before we can believe He has the desire and power to change us.

2. God brought each person to a place of acknowledging with honesty the nature of his heart and the need in his life to recognize his true unredeemed name, as it were. Jacob had to confess that he was a schemer. Abraham and Sarah lived in rueful recognition of their own inadequacy. Peter saw how changeable he was. Paul in a blinding instant was shown the potential for self-destruction that lay within his heart if he followed the path of his namesake Saul. Each had to assess himself in some way. Paul Tournier writes in *The Meaning of Persons*, "It is before God, who knows us and loves us and forgives, that we dare to see ourselves as we are."

3. Except for Paul, who chose his own name, God revealed to each of them the prophetic new name, the glimpse of the new identity that would be theirs under His healing and restoring hand. And all five, including Paul, found that with this new name came a sense of their place in the Kingdom of God. Abraham and Sarah caught the vision of their place as the father and mother of the believers to come; Jacob came to understand his pivotal role in establishing the tribes of the nation that would bear his new name. Peter knew that someday he would be an anchor for his fellow disciples, and Paul was told explicitly of the suffering he would share with Christ.

4. God infused them with His Spirit and as their relationship with Him continued, each took on more and more of His divine nature. God brought Abraham and Sarah from barrenness into miraculous fertility. He transformed Jacob from

conniver to patriarch by giving him the integrity and self-control of the Holy Spirit. Into Peter, God injected steadfast-ness and compassion, and into the arrogant Paul, a divine humility.

5. God ordered their circumstances (both blessings and trials) to bring these new names into reality. Sarah and Abraham were given an heir and then were called to sacrifice that promise back to Him. Jacob was allowed to prosper and obtain his heart's desire, and then his hip was put out of joint. Peter was loved, singled out, trained, broken by his own betrayal of Jesus, then restored and commissioned. Paul, through all the suffering he was ordained to endure, was blessed with the closest of relationships with the Person he loved most dearly.

Note especially that each set of circumstances was as unique as the person God was fashioning.

6. The result in all their lives was that, even though they all were dealt with in basically the same way, and all partook of the nature of God, they all retained their individuality. In fact, we might say that their true colors grew only more vivid as they yielded themselves to God for His purposes.

COMMON DENOMINATORS: TRAITS

In addition to finding a pattern in the way God works to give us new identities, we can also see traits that each of these people had in common, qualities that made them malleable in God's hands:

1. They were thirsty for truth. In the midst of a sophisti-cated, comfortable existence, Abraham was looking for some-thing more than the Chaldean idolatry represented, and his ears were open to the voice that called him. Jacob, as we have seen, fervently wanted the blessings of God in his life. Peter and his compatriots were looking for the Messiah with all the longing that centuries of oppression could produce. And Paul was doing all he could to win the favor of a God he thought he knew. These were people on the lookout for

reality, aliens and exiles whose hearts ached for some half-remembered home.

2. They were capable of passionate love. Abraham was able to lay that which he loved best upon the altar because he trusted and loved the One who had given it to him. Peter's love for Jesus propelled him out of boats, and Paul's enabled him to call his life of hardship "a slight momentary affliction." Even Jacob, perhaps the most unappealing of characters, showed, in his love for Rachel, his ability to give his heart away. The capacity for deep feeling, even if it is negative, is something God can work with; Jesus in Revelation 3:16 calls for us to be either hot or cold. The lukewarm He will spit out of His mouth.

3. They acted on what they believed. The people we have considered were not spectators, content to give mere intellectual assent to what God told them was true. The miracle of Isaac's birth called for human participation; Abraham and Sarah, as foolish as they may have felt, came together in faith. Jacob dared to face his vengeful brother after coming face to face with God. At Jesus' Word, Peter stepped out on an element he knew for a fact would not hold him, and Paul staked everything he possessed on a heavenly vision. They acted upon what God told them was so, and found in the doing that it *was* so.

If we have these qualities, we too can enter into our new identities.

3

THE GIVER

As a child I was raised on such Cecil B. De Mille biblical epics as *The Ten Commandments* and *Samson and Delilah*. From those movies, I learned that when God was about to speak to His people or intervene in their lives, the harmonies of a full mixed chorus would begin and a shaft of light would break upon the person about to be spoken to. In church I would from time to time glance up hopefully at the nearest stained glass window and listen hard for the angelic humming to begin. . . . But deep in my heart I thought: That was then; this is now. God talked to spiritual giants like Abraham and Paul. But me?

Many people share my former skepticism. Yes, it happened in the Bible, they think. But does it really happen today? Isn't it presumptuous to think that God knows and cares about me? If not, can I dare to believe that He has a plan for me and my life? Is it really His desire to give me a new identity? To believe that God's promise is still true, we must understand two things: the nature of God Himself, and the nature of His Word, the Bible.

GOD'S NATURE

Let's look at five character traits that help us understand God's nature and how it affects our identities.

HE IS CHANGELESS

We can know that God will deal with us as He dealt with Abraham and Peter and the rest, because He does not change. It is true that we have seen Him manifest Himself throughout the centuries in different ways: as Father, Son, and Holy Spirit. And yet the central tenet of our Judeo-Christian heritage, "Hear, O Israel: The Lord our God is one Lord" (Deuteronomy 6:4), means that God is unified, one in essence, though manifest in three Persons. The Scriptures assert that God *cannot* change. In Malachi 3:6, for example, He says of Himself, "I the Lord do not change." Psalm 33:11 declares, "The counsel of the Lord stands for ever, the thoughts of his heart to all generations." This is in contrast to the heavens, which themselves are "the work of thy hands. They will perish, but thou dost endure; they will all wear out like a garment. Thou changest them like raiment, and they pass away; but thou art the same, and thy years have no end" (Psalm 102:25–27).

Neither does He change in character. James called Him "the father of lights with whom there is no variation or shadow due to change" (James 1:17). Hebrews 13:8 says explicitly: "Jesus Christ is the same yesterday and today and for ever."

And what does this have to do with our new name? *We can*

count on His purposes, His desires for us, and His ways of shaping us to fit our new names as being in line with what we have seen in Scripture.

HE IS IMPARTIAL

Peter learned that "God is no respecter of persons" when the Holy Spirit was poured out upon the Roman centurion and his family (see Acts 10:34). James corroborated that by admonishing those who bore God's name never to show partiality among fellow believers (James 2:1). Indeed, in the Old Testament Law, God told the people He was forming to show His character to the world that He didn't want them to pervert justice in *any* way: "You shall do no injustice in judgment; you shall not be partial to the poor or defer to the great" (Leviticus 19:15), an interesting warning in this day of liberal attempts to rectify past injustices by tipping the scales in the other direction. Because God is not willing that *any* should perish, He has said that all who will may come to Him; in Jeremiah 29:13, He promised that He would be found by those who search for Him with their whole hearts. And in Isaiah 55:1–3, He issued a universal invitation:

> *"Ho, every one who thirsts, come to the waters; and he who has no money, come, buy and eat! Come, buy wine and milk without money and without price. Why do you spend your money for that which is not bread, and your labor for that which does not satisfy? Hearken diligently to me, and eat what is good, and delight yourselves in fatness. Incline your ear, and come to me; hear, that your soul may live; and I will make with you an everlasting covenant, my steadfast, sure love for David."*

HE IS OMNISCIENT

God knows and loves us all because He is our Creator. In John 1:47, when Jesus met the young Nathanael, He greeted him, "An Israelite indeed, in whom is no guile" (a punning reference to the original Israel—Jacob—who was very guileful indeed). When Nathanael asked, "How do you know me?" Jesus astounded him by referring to a time when Nathanael had been alone, probably meditating. It was enough to convince him that this rabbi was the Messiah. We can almost hear Jesus laughing as He challenges: "Because I said to you, I saw you under the fig tree, do you believe? You shall see greater things than these!" I like to imagine Nathanael's surprise if Jesus had told him how long He had really known him. . . .

The prophet Jeremiah shared the revelation God gave him concerning God's foreknowledge of him:

> *"Before I formed you in the womb I knew you, and before you were born I consecrated you; I appointed you a prophet to the nations."*
> Jeremiah 1:5

Paul also understood the prescient love of God for His people:

> *Blessed be the God and Father of our Lord Jesus Christ, who has blessed us in Christ with every spiritual blessing in the heavenly places, even as he chose us in him* before the foundation of the world, *that we should be holy and blameless before him.*
> Ephesians 1:3–4

Paul again spoke of our having been destined and appointed to live for the praise of His glory in Ephesians 1:12. Further, he explained to the Ephesian believers that "we are his workmanship [literally, His "poems"], created in Christ Jesus for good works, which God prepared beforehand, that we should walk in them" (Ephesians 2:10).

It was to David, however, that God gave the deepest revelation of the truth that "it is he that made us, and we are his" (Psalm 100:3). In Psalm 139, David pondered the wondrous thought that God knows us inside and out, before and behind; that He knows our conversation "even before a word is on my tongue" that He is "acquainted with all [our] ways," when we sit down and when we rise up. The reason for God's omniscience?

> *For thou didst form my inward parts, thou didst knit me together in my mother's womb. . . . Thy eyes beheld my unformed substance; in thy book were written, every one of them, the days that were formed for me, when as yet there was none of them.*   Psalm 139:13, 16

HE IS A GOD OF INDIVIDUALS

The psalmist in Psalm 147:4 tells us that God "determines the number of the stars, he gives to all of them their names." Jesus assures us that at any given moment God knows the number of hairs on every human head (Matthew 10:30).

This is an astonishing thought, one that is central to inheriting our new names: God knows every individual as intimately as He knew the prophets and kings and martyrs of the Bible. Even David in the midst of divine revelation admitted that such "high knowledge" was beyond his comprehension (Psalm 139:6). So how shall *we* come to an understanding and acceptance that God can and does know us as well as He knew the giants on the spiritual landscape? In light of the billions of people who have inhabited this planet for all its centuries, how can I believe He even knows that I exist?

If we have ever begun to read the Bible from cover to cover, chances are we did fine until about the tenth chapter of Genesis where the "begats" begin, the genealogical lists full of unpronounceable names. We may bravely pick up again at chapter 11 and proceed, soon finding great mountains of strange names again in the first eight or nine chapters of 1 Chronicles. Although these are but lists to us, to God each of these names signifies a person, a creature with a destiny, a "holy particularity of soul" to use Douglas Steere's wonderful phrase. Often on an airplane, I have looked down over the sprawling landscape of Dallas or the cramped spires of New

York and have pondered the complexity represented by the tiny figures inching along the major highways. How can God contain all this knowledge?

In John 10 God explained this in familiar terms by drawing an analogy of a good shepherd. Though to another, sheep are just a "herd," to the shepherd they are individual animals with distinct personalities, idiosyncrasies, and needs. In today's terms, we might recall that a tiny microchip can store billions of units of information and try to reason from that fact the capacity of an infinite God. But God is not simply the repository of facts.

In trying to grasp how He is a God of individuals, a far warmer analogy might be to consider ourselves at Christmastime. To a stranger, our Christmas lists would probably be meaningless. If you were to find mine dropped on the floor of the local shopping mall, the names Michael, Meg, Kit, Phil, Agnes, Hank, Steve, Sue, Terry, Todd, Daniel, David, Sarah, Katy would be just names. To me, these are faces, relationships, mannerisms, characteristics, qualities of heart, memories, laughter, tastes, preferences, sounds, smells, sights. If we as humans can store so much about so many in our hearts, why do we doubt the capacity of the heart of God?

But surely, we think, there must be a hierarchy of some kind in God's heart. How can He *not* show favoritism? How can He possibly have room, even in His giant heart, for all the billions who've lived. . . .?

He helped me begin to understand these mysteries through a friend's experience. Gerry became very anxious before the birth of her second child. Her first was the apple of her eye, her delight, and she was afraid that she couldn't possibly make room in her heart for the newcomer. As she lay in joyful exhaustion after the delivery, her husband asked, "Have you made room for this one?" "No," she replied. "I grew a new heart!" God has a heart for each one of us. As Jesus put it, "In my Father's house are many rooms" (John 14:2), places especially prepared for all who will come.

HE IS OMNIPOTENT

The people of Nazareth made a grave error when they continued to regard Jesus as "a hometown boy." Because He had grown up in their midst, they could not look past the familiar external face and form and into the realm of the divine life within Him, out of which His gracious words came. Many today who have grown up with the Sunday school idea of "gentle Jesus, meek and mild," may readily accept the idea that God understands and has compassion for our problems. Yet we may subconsciously doubt His ability to change us. We may ask with Jeremiah, "Can the Ethiopian change his skin or the leopard his spots?" (Jeremiah 13:23). We wonder, can God really straighten out my twisted perceptions, heal my broken heart, erase my pride, deliver me from my jealousy, redeem my anger, rechannel my zeal, *give* me zeal in the first place?

By asking such questions, we show that we have forgotten that He is a sovereign Lord over us and over every circumstance that comes into our daily lives. We have not yet glimpsed the glorified Lord, the sight of whose majesty caused John, His disciple, to fall on his face, stricken:

> *I saw seven golden lampstands, and in the midst of the lampstands one like a son of man, clothed with a long robe and with a golden girdle round his breast; his head and his hair were white as white wool, white as snow; his eyes were like a flame of fire, his feet were like burnished bronze, refined as in a furnace, and his voice was like the sound of many waters . . . and his face was like the sun shining in full strength.*   Revelation 1:12–16

We do not know in our hearts that with God, "nothing will be impossible," as Gabriel assured Mary (Luke 1:37). In short, if we do not know His power, we do not yet know His name.

The first word used for God in the Bible—"In the beginning *God* created the heavens and the earth" (Genesis 1:1)—is *Elohim*, which means "the great energy ones."[1] It is a plural

word, but it is linked with a singular verb, for it reflects the
mysterious nature of the Godhead: three Persons, Father,
Son, and Holy Spirit, united in essence as one. This Energy
Source, if you will, *creates* (literally, "brings out of nothing").
In contrast, "creative" human beings merely form from what
is already available. The very first sentence in Scripture,
then, informs us that God is beyond beginnings, the source
of all power, the Mind and Heart from whom all that we
know or imagine has sprung.

The tender, merciful Father is also the omnipotent God. As
we have seen, *El Shaddai*, friend and nurturer, is first the
Almighty One. The mother-hen image that Jesus used in
expressing His sorrow over stubborn Jerusalem should not
cancel out the awesome memory of Mt. Sinai. The "still,
small voice" can also thunder, striking terror in the hearts of
the proud. And the Jesus with whom we can so readily
identify in His humanity is no longer the crucified carpenter
of Nazareth. His name (that is, His position, His authority) is
now above every name. He is in His glory. His full blossoming and His power are limitless: Even the demons know who
is Lord, and shudder (James 2:19)!

Scripture is full of declarations of His power over creation—
the wind, the snow, the sea, the heavens, the grass, the sun,
the moon and the stars—and over the animals—the whale
and the sparrow, the lion and the lambs.

But most pertinent, the Bible tells of His power to know
and work within the sacred ground of the human heart
through His Holy Spirit. In the first chapter of Acts, as the
disciples pray for Him to show who among them He wants to
take Judas' place, they pray to the "Lord, who knowest the
hearts of all men" (Acts 1:24). In the original Greek, this
expression is actually a title, sounding like the name of a
knight in an allegory: Lord Heartknower.[2] And indeed, the
Lord Jesus Christ alone has those eyes ("like a flame of fire")
to penetrate into the depths of human motives.

We cannot know hearts—most especially our own. We
cannot see truth through the tangled fabric of motivations,

memories, extenuating circumstances, efforts that went awry, hurts, fears, bruises, and scar tissue. Nor can we change hearts, though we coax, cajole, wheedle, nag, manipulate. But He can. This is God's exclusive territory. Even those who do not acknowledge Him are under His influence. As Solomon observed, "The king's heart is a stream of water in the hand of the Lord; he turns it wherever he will" (Proverbs 21:1). How much more can He work in us "both to will and to work for his good pleasure" (Philippians 2:13) when we *invite* Him in to establish His Lordship in our hearts?

Again we may hesitate, thinking to ourselves, I've been responding to things this way, failing that way for thirty-five or forty years. How can I be changed overnight? This habit is so engrained, this wound has festered for so long, this feeling's so entrenched. . . . I've always been this way.

God is not limited by time or space, not bound by cause and effect as we perceive it. He is not constrained by the perimeters of human deduction. To God, "one day is as a thousand years, and a thousand years as one day" (2 Peter 3:8). The woman ill with an issue of blood for twelve years (Luke 8), the man blind from birth (John 9), the lame man, lying helpless by the healing waters of Bethesda for thirty-eight years (John 5)—all were healed in a moment of time.

THE NATURE OF GOD'S WORD

We may already see how to apply universal laws like the Ten Commandments ("Thou shall not kill") or the ethical instructions of the New Testament ("Bear one another's burdens"). We may have no trouble believing that such rules speak to modern human experience. But we may find it more difficult to look to personal stories (rather than Laws and Principles) for instruction in God's ways for us. There seems to be a great divide that keeps us from relating the lives of biblical people to our own. Yet, their stories set precedents for our lives as we search for our identities.

Paul, writing to Timothy, insisted:

All scripture is inspired by God and profitable for teaching, for reproof, for correction, and for training in righteousness, that the man of God may be complete, equipped for every good work.
                                                                    2 Timothy 3:16

Paul was referring not to the New Testament, of course, or only to that portion of the Old Testament we know as the Law. He was talking about the major portion of the Old Testament which is, in fact, story after story of a personal God touching and changing individual human hearts: shepherds, harlots, farmers, warriors, cowards, and kings. Paul, Timothy, and all their contemporaries prized the histories of those who had walked with God, for they knew that because God's purposes were consistent from generation to generation, they could look to these stories as providing models for their own lives. As Paul said, that's what they are there for!

David essentially said the same thing. Praising God's Word in Psalm 119, he declared that he cherished such stories for their wisdom: "Thy testimonies are my delight, they are my counselors" (verse 24). He also used them to teach others: "Let those who fear thee turn to me, that they may know thy testimonies" (verse 79). Because God's testimonies were his "meditation," David claimed more understanding than his teachers and even the aged (verses 99–100). And in Psalm 22 he wrote how he comforted himself in extreme affliction with a rehearsal of God's faithfulness to his ancestors, the children of Israel.

David was bold enough to examine God's ways with others and to apply them to himself and his fellow believers. Peter, in his Pentecost sermon, declared that God's promise of a new life "is to you and to your children and to all that are far off, every one whom the Lord our God calls to him" (Acts 2:39). Testimonies through the subsequent centuries have shown that God's Word continues to be applicable. With the boldness given us by the Holy Spirit, we can expect God's purpose and ways to be the same in our lives today as they have always been, for His Word is eternally and universally true.

GOD'S PURPOSES IN HIS WORD

We can know that He desires to rescue us from our old identities partly, of course, through watching what He has already done for thousands of years, as seen in the personal stories we have already studied. But the Bible also contains prophecies and parables expressing this rescuing purpose. The prophecies begin at the Fall itself when God, even as He had to close off the Garden, promised Adam and Eve that their salvation would be coming through the seed of a woman (Genesis 3:15), a prophetic clue to the supernatural birth of His Son (see Galatians 4:4). Through the patriarchs, as we have seen, and through Moses, He renewed His promise—not only *shown* through men's lives but also *stated*—the promise of a new godly character: "All the peoples of the earth shall see that you are called by the name of the Lord" (Deuteronomy 28:10).

These promises of renewal are frequent and richly varied. Sometimes they come in the form of a living parable: In the book of Nehemiah we can see in the rebuilding of Jerusalem one such living parable of the work of the Holy Spirit in repairing ruined personalities. Sometimes they come poetically: Psalm 107 celebrates and catalogues the varied "lost souls" whom God has redeemed—the sick, the wanderers, the homeless, the rebels, the prisoners, the needy. Sometimes they come as visions: Through Ezekiel's vision in the valley of the dry bones (Ezekiel 37:11–14), God shows His power to bring back to life that which, like our spirits, is dead and dry. And in the heartbreaking life of the prophet Hosea, who loved, lost, and ransomed back his promiscuous wife Gomer, we see in another living parable the kind of deathless love that causes God to reclaim even the most "damaged goods."

Through Jeremiah He promises a future of new hearts and
spirits, "a future and a hope" (Jeremiah 29:11), and through
Joel He swears to redeem the havoc wreaked by our past: "I
will restore to you the years which the swarming locust has
eaten" (Joel 2:25). In Isaiah 40:3–5, we find the poetic
promise by which John the Baptist announced the work of
the Lord: to sanctify, to heal, to straighten out the human
personality, twisted by sin. Again, through Isaiah, the Lord
promises His people who are "trapped in holes and hidden
in prisons" (Isaiah 42:22), that He will restore them.

Best of all, God promises to minister to His people Himself.
Sick of false prophets and uncaring priests, He vowed:

> *I myself will be the shepherd of my sheep, and I will make them lie
> down, says the Lord God. I will seek the lost, and I will bring back
> the strayed, and I will bind up the crippled, and I will strengthen the
> weak, and the fat and the strong I will watch over; I will feed them
> in justice.*   Ezekiel 34:15–16

GOD'S GREATEST WORD

So we have seen that God has shown His desires in such a
variety of ways that it would seem impossible to miss His
intent. He wants to redeem us and give us each a new
identity. But the greatest of His expressions of yearning for
us came in His own Son. It is in the Lord Jesus Christ Himself
that we have God's promise to heal and make us truly
ourselves, truly fulfilled in the flesh. In the God-Man Jesus,
we have the likeness of God (2 Corinthians 4:4), the One who
carries the glory of God in His face, and the promise for
mankind that we will be changed into His likeness (2
Corinthians 3:18).

In Jesus' first sermon in His hometown synagogue, He
arose and turned in the Scriptures to the book of Isaiah: "The
Spirit of the Lord is upon me, because he has anointed me to
preach good news to the poor. He has sent me to proclaim
release to the captives and recovering of sight to the blind, to

set at liberty those who are oppressed, to proclaim the acceptable year of the Lord" (Luke 4:18–19).

The divine intention is not to restore the environment, or to establish a perfect system of government, or even to eradicate evil—in *this* world. Jesus is announcing a jubilee: freedom for every individual from the blinding, crippling, ultimately fatal prison of self. He has come to seek and save the lost (Luke 19:10).

In a series of parables (Luke 15:3–32), the Lord Jesus gives us a picture of God's joy in finding and restoring His lost creatures: The housewife calling all her friends and neighbors to celebrate finding one lost coin, although she had nine others; the shepherd, with a flock of one hundred sheep, whose heart is with the one that is lost, who rejoices when he finds the wandering one and carries it home on his shoulders; and the father, whose ungrateful, rebellious son finally comes to his senses after wasting all that he has on the pleasures of the world.

In this story, the father evidently has been on the lookout since the boy's departure, for Scripture says he saw him "while he was yet at a distance . . . and had compassion, and ran and embraced him and kissed him" (Luke 15:20). Then to the one who has squandered his original inheritance (even as we, each one, have to some degree wasted ours) the father gives a robe ("the best robe"), a ring for his hand, and shoes for his feet—all symbolic of the total restoration of his place, his authority, in other words, his "name" as a welcome and beloved son. We may, like the older brother, struggle to comprehend the kind of love that is so merciful and generous to such a sinner; nevertheless, that is the portrait of our God He wants us to have.

As powerful as these illustrations are, there is something far more expressive than teachings, far more informative even than the reams of prophecy, the symbols and types and foreshadowings, the glimpses of God's face that came before: The single most powerful expression of God's lovingkindness toward us is the Person of the Lord Jesus Christ. For in

Him—in His actions, His responses, His flesh-and-blood reality—we can *know* that God knows our condition, for He has lived it Himself! "The Word became flesh and dwelt among us," John marvels in the opening verses of his Gospel (John 1:14). In his letters, he harkens to the disciples' relationship with Jesus, and he is still awed by his experience: "The life was made manifest, and we saw it" (1 John 1:2).

Through the Gospels we get a full picture of Jesus' humanity. Born a normal little helpless human baby into a poor but honorable family, He lived the life of a boy of His time, enjoying the sun, feeling the wind and rain as He ran and played with His friends. He learned obedience and how to balance His obligations to His earthly parents. He "grew in stature" (literally, "advanced," as a pioneer would go into new territory), struggling with the same physical and emotional pressures of any other young man approaching adulthood. As He entered His adult ministry, weakened by forty days of fasting, He endured the first of many onslaughts from Satan, insidious temptations designed to pique His spiritual ambition, His innate human altruism.

As He grew in fame, He suffered the fickleness of the crowds that vacillated between adulation and hostility, an almost total lack of privacy, the constant nattering of the scribes, the snide and patronizing comments of the Pharisees, the suspicions and jealousy of the religious leaders. He heard His Word as it had come down through the centuries misapplied, watched it strangled into deadly ritual and rule, and then saw it disobeyed, disregarded by the leaders. He was drained of power as He healed, felt loneliness even with numerous companions (for who around Him yet had more than an infant's capacity for spiritual things?), and knew what it was to conquer temptations of the flesh only to face temptations of the spirit, to absorb day after day of frustration and interruption, the kind of stress we tend to claim as peculiarly twentieth-century pressure. His family doubted His sanity, His hometown scorned Him, His friends misunderstood His mission, His disciples deserted, and one deliberately betrayed Him. In Gethsemane, preparing to receive the tidal wave of universal and eternal sin that rolled toward Him, He sweat blood as He struggled to accept the cup He had been handed.

And finally—on the cross—He experienced the worst facet of the human condition of all: to be utterly cut off from, alienated from, cast out of the presence of God; to be without any solace or comfort or security, plunged to the depths of a palpable darkness, thick with howling demons and the full force of hell's minions. He tasted the shattered condition of a human personality separated from God. He who had been with the Word, who Himself *was* the Word, wrenched by human sin away from all, He was ripped from His Father like the Temple veil, for love of the humans who killed Him.

Because of these experiences, the Gospels tell us that when Jesus saw people suffering in *any* kind of sorrow or oppression, physical or mental (see Matthew 9:36; Mark 8:2; Luke 7:13), He had "compassion" on them. In the Greek, *splagch-nizesthai*, a powerful word, means "to be moved with pity to the innermost parts of one's body, to the very depths of one's being." William Barclay points out that, unlike us, Jesus was never annoyed, exasperated, repelled, or disgusted by laziness, disease, lostness, and hunger. He felt sorry for His people. He literally ached for them. The extraordinary thing about the use of this term *compassion* is that it is being applied to someone who is divine.

As Barclay explains it, the Stoics reasoned that God's supreme characteristic was *apatheia*, the condition of being totally unaffected by another being, least of all by one's inferiors. If I cause you to have joy or sorrow, the Stoics would say, I momentarily have power over you. Since God is all-powerful, then it would follow that He must be *unable* to feel, since to feel our sorrow would be to suffer momentary loss of power to us.

Pagan religious thought believed in a God whose essence was that he was incapable of feeling pity; pagan

ethics taught that the aim of life was a life from which all
pity and all compassion were totally and finally ban-
ished. The idea of a God who could be moved with
compassion, and of a life whose motive force was
pitying love, must have come to such a world literally
like a new revelation. We think it a commonplace that
God is love, and that the Christian life is love. We would
do well to remember that we would never have known
that without the revelation of Jesus Christ, of whom it is
so often and so amazingly said that He was moved with
compassion.[3]

To try to sum up the attributes of our God would be an
impossible and presumptuous task; even to list all of the
names He has revealed to His people through the centuries—
the Almighty, the Provider, the Healer, the Sustainer, the
One who hears, the Alpha and the Omega—would not be
sufficient. Isaiah was right in declaring His name "Wonderful" (Isaiah 9:6), for He is indeed "singular, difficult,
hidden, and great"; He far surpasses the scope of even the
most exalted of our human words. Suffice it to say that the
God with whom we are in relationship is the same God who
called the whole world into being with a phrase, who
sustains the universe daily by His constant fiat (Hebrews
1:3), and who can call things that are not (yet) as if they were
(Romans 4:17). Our God can meet Simon and call him Peter.
This is He who calls us by name.

4

THE GIVING OF
YOUR "FAMILY" NAME

I call you by your name, I surname you. . . .   Isaiah 45:4

If throughout history God's Word reveals His promise to redeem us—give us a new name—what is the first step we must take toward claiming that promise? It is to look at ourselves honestly and acknowledge our real condition.

The beginning of a new name comes when a human being encounters the Lord, and, seeing God's holiness for the first time, realizes his own sinfulness and his need for a new identity. We see this acknowledgment of sinfulness time and again with the great men of Scripture. Isaiah, confronted with the vision of Jehovah, His regal train filling the Temple (Isaiah 6:1–5), fell down and confessed his human impurity: "I am a man of unclean lips." Moses removed his shoes to acknowledge the awesome reality of One whose very presence caused a bush to burst into flames, yet did not consume it (Exodus 3:2). Jacob was thrilled with fear at the realization that heaven pervaded the world around him and that God had been near him all his life. Paul met the risen Lord and was literally knocked off his horse, blind and utterly undone.

Jesus observed that the physician only comes to those who recognize their sickness and call for him (Matthew 9:12); likewise, only those who see their need for salvation will cry out for a savior. The prerequisite to Jacob's receiving his new name—an honest confession of his old one—is required of all who come to repentance. All who rest comfortably with their own standards of "relative righteousness" ("Well, at least I'm better than so-and-so over there!") remain blind to their own need.

The genesis of a new name, then, is the kind of encounter with God that stuns the proud spirit, disclosing the sickness and need within us.

But not all encounters are confrontations like Paul's. We may meet God in the heart-piercing power of a miracle in our lives: Peter, hauling up his splitting nets, cried out to Jesus: "Depart from me, for I am a sinful man" (Luke 5:8). Like the Prodigal Son we may recognize our lifestyle as "eating husks" and remember the richness of our father's house (Luke 15:16). Or like the centurion on execution detail, we may catch a glimpse of God's indescribable love on the cross, see in its reflection our interminable selfishness and fall to our knees (Luke 23:47). Or a life-changing encounter may come as we experience His faithful providence; that is, our needs may dawn on us as we are exposed to the truth of God's Word.

This recognition of truth, which drives us to our knees, was probably what sent the teacher Nicodemus scurrying at night to question the young rabbi, Jesus of Nazareth, and it was to him that Jesus began to spell out God's eternal plan of redemption, a plan that had been encoded in every law, every sacrifice, every strange and intricate direction God had given to His people for centuries.

Jesus chose a story from the Old Testament to illustrate this interlocking truth to Nicodemus: During their time in the wilderness, the children of Israel had been bitten by poisonous snakes. God had instructed Moses to make a bronze replica of the serpent and lift it up for the people to gaze upon if they were bitten. All those who obeyed this strange command would be cured. And so it was (Numbers 21:6–9). Jesus explained: "And as Moses lifted up the serpent in the wilderness, so must the Son of man be lifted up, that whoever believes in him may have eternal life" (John 3:14–15). In His death upon the cross Jesus would be taking onto Himself the penalty God was obliged by His righteousness to exact for sin, absorbing, as it were, the poison of sin, so that His people might live. By receiving this mighty act of God on our behalf, we do not perish, but instead receive His life.

JOINING OUR LIVES TO GOD'S

Nicodemus was chosen by Jesus to hear, also, the mysterious explanation of what happens *after* our knees buckle in the clear light of our own sinfulness. We are ready then to take on an entirely new identity, by joining our lives to His. To enter God's Kingdom, Jesus told Nicodemus, you must be born anew—born from above. You must become a new creature, take on an entirely new identity, created not by human birth, not by one's own will, nor by the resolution of flesh and blood, but by the Spirit of God. Just as He had become incarnate in the womb of a young girl of the tribe of Judah, so God Himself would be born in us. He would dwell in our midst, more precisely within each one who received Him. This was His plan from the beginning, the mystery for ages and generations (Colossians 1:26).

The joining of God's life to ours is expressed many ways in Scripture. Jesus says in Revelation 3:20: "Behold, I stand at the door and knock; if any one hears my voice and opens the door, I will come in to him and eat with him, and he with me." To His disciples He described it another way: "I am the vine, you are the branches" (John 15:5).

Paul expressed this union from the human point of view:

> *I have been crucified with Christ; it is no longer I who live, but Christ who lives in me; and the life I now live in the flesh I live by faith in the Son of God, who loved me and gave himself for me.*
>
> Galatians 2:20

To the Philippians Paul wrote: "I can do all things in him who strengthens me," literally, "who infuses me with his strength" (Philippians 4:13). Bible teacher Malcolm Smith likens this infusion to the process by which water and coffee grounds, two separate and different things, are fused together in percolation, creating an entirely new substance.

Dr. Paul Brand, in his book *Fearfully and Wonderfully Made*, compares it to the process by which DNA passes on an infallible identity to each new cell:

> Christ has infused us with spiritual life that is just as real as natural life. I may sometimes doubt my new identity . . . but the Bible statements are unequivocal. "Whoever believes in the Son has eternal life," said Jesus, "but whoever rejects the Son will not see life" (John 3:36). The difference between a person joined to Christ and one not joined to Him is as striking as the difference between a dead tissue and my organic body. DNA has organized chemicals and minerals to form a living, growing body, all of whose parts possess its unique corporate identity. In a parallel way, God uses the materials and genes of natural man, splitting them apart and recombining them with His own spiritual life. . . . And now, through union with Him, I can carry within me the literal presence of God . . . not just the image of, or the philosophy of, or faith in, but the actual substance of God.[1]

OUR POSITION IN CHRIST

Being born again, organically joined to the person and life flow of God, naturally gives us a new relationship to Him. Second Corinthians 5:17 says of those in Christ: "Old things [literally, positions] have passed away, and the new has come." Galatians 4:4–5 expresses our new creaturehood in terms of adoption into God's family: "But when the time had fully come, God sent forth His Son, born of a woman, born under the law, to redeem those who were under the law, so that we might receive adoption as sons."

Anyone in Christ is declared a saint—regarded as such by God according to the sinlessness of Jesus Christ—by virtue of having been redeemed by His blood. We are counted perfect as He is perfect, set apart as He is set apart from all that is not of God. We have been cleansed, forgiven, and justified from sin. We have been given the indwelling Spirit, the gift of eternal life, and have become legal heirs of God's. We are fully accepted as a part of the Beloved, as members of His mystical Body, and His Bride. Finally, believers are, in a real but almost incomprehensible sense, already raised with Christ, awaiting only the transformation of our earthly bodies to glorified ones, like the Lord's own resurrection body.

These promises are as true for the newest and weakest believer as for the oldest and strongest, for they are based on the merit of our Savior, not our own. The Corinthians, we know, were egregiously unholy in some areas of life (see 1 Corinthians 5:1–2; 6:1–8), yet they are referred to as "saints" (1 Corinthians 1:2, 6:11). By the same token we too can share that name. Though many of these truths may seem "too high" for attaining, as David expressed it, nevertheless they are the promises of God's own Word. Knowledge of our status in God's sight should, to believing hearts, be an inspiration to live in fact what we have been called to by position.

This new status gives all of us who recognize our "cho-
senness" a special, *collective* identity in Christ, and it is
important for us to understand what is ours simply by virtue
of belonging to that family.

WE ARE BELOVED IN CHRIST

Because believers are actually *in* Christ, we can partake of
the Father's love, His deepest affection and approval, which
rests upon the Lord Jesus. Likewise, we can now be so bold
as to store in our hearts the declarations of love that Jesus in
turn expresses toward us. In the Song of Solomon, the
Bridegroom King estimates the preciousness of his Bride:
"Behold, you are beautiful, my love, behold, you are beautiful!" (4:1). The King calls us to commune with Him: "O my
dove, in the clefts of the rock, in the covert of the cliff, let me
see your face, let me hear your voice, for your voice is sweet,
and your face is comely" (2:14). When the Bride protests her
"darkness," a symbol for what we would call our unworthiness because of sin, the King protests: "You are all fair, my
love; there is no flaw in you" (4:7). He further expresses His
feeling for us in words full of heart-melting vulnerability:
"You have ravished my heart, my sister, my bride, you have
ravished my heart with a glance of your eyes . . ."(4:9).

In Isaiah 43:4, God says to us: "You are precious in my
eyes, and honored, and I love you." Through the prophet
Zephaniah He reveals a picture of the fervent pleasure He
takes in us: "The Lord, your God, is in your midst, a warrior
who gives victory; he will rejoice over you with gladness, he
will renew you in his love; he will exult over you with loud
singing as on a day of festival" (3:17–18). Psalm 17:8 and
Deuteronomy 32:10 both speak of our being "the apple of
God's eye." (This idiomatic rendering of the Hebrew word
ishon, "little man," refers to the image that falls upon the
retina as one person gazes at another.)

God expresses His relationship to us in a variety of
nurturing metaphors, all fueled by a love that is simulta-

neously jealous, tender, and faithful. In one small passage of the book of Hosea alone He likens himself to a mother teaching her child to walk, a husband binding his wife with cords of love as in a wedding dance, and as a farmer leading his tired oxen to pasture and rest (Hosea 11:3–4).

Certainly God's highest commendation of us is that He regards us as His inheritance: "For the Lord's portion is his people" (Deuteronomy 32:9). The significance of this statement deepens when we recognize what it foreshadows: We are the prize for which God's only Son went to the cross. In the Messianic passages of Isaiah 53 we are called "the fruit" of the travail of His soul, and we are told that He will be satisfied with it (verse 11). In Hebrews 12:2 we are "the joy that was set before him," and in Hebrews 2:10 we are told that it was to bring us to glory that He suffered the ineffable agony and shame of a sinner's death. The apostle John explains that we love Him only "because he first loved us" (1 John 4:19).

Perhaps the richest and most concise description of God's perspective on us is expressed in 1 Peter 2:9:

> But you are a chosen race, a royal priesthood, a holy nation, God's own people, that you may declare the wonderful deeds of him who called you out of darkness into his marvelous light.

Take by word and phrase this description sums up the new position and purpose of those who have received Jesus Christ as Savior.

WE ARE A CHOSEN RACE

The word *chosen*, "to select for favor," is rich with meaning; basically, it suggests that we have been known, designed, redeemed, and called out. We are known by God because we existed first in His *Logos* or Word, that is, the idea from which the entire creation came into being.

Also, each of us is individually chosen, destined for a particular purpose, for a particular moment in time and space. The Old Testament book of Esther tells the story of the beautiful Jewish girl Hadassah who is taken into the harem of the Persian King Xerxes and is subsequently made his queen. A pogrom against the Jews is threatened, and her uncle-guardian Mordecai pleads with Hadassah (now called Esther) to use her position to save her people. He argues that if she fails, deliverance will come some other way, but he presses, "Who knows whether you have not come to the kingdom for such a time as this?" (Esther 4:14). All that had gone into Esther—her beauty, her heritage, her position—had been carefully designed by God for just that moment in history.

The staggering fact is that the same is true for each of us.

We have been called by name. Even as the boy Samuel was awakened in the night by the sound of God calling his name, so God has spoken to each of us in the darkness of our hearts, calling us in such a way that we recognize His voice.

But called *to* what, *for* what? Primarily, it means that we have been invited to partake of the blessing of redemption, to sit down at the King's banquet table. It also means called away from some other pursuit. The Greek word *ekklesia*, from which we get our word for *church*, means literally the "called-out" ones. God will not allow our hearts, like Lot's wife, to stay focused on the world; He calls us to spend our attention, our energy, our love, and loyalty not on this world but on His heavenly Kingdom. As Noah was called out of the world to find refuge in the ark, so we are to enter a relationship with God through our ark, Jesus Christ.

It is interesting that Peter writes these encouraging words to the Diaspora—believers scattered by persecution. "Beloved," he writes, "we are aliens and exiles." The words still apply. The pull of the Holy Spirit is always toward a heavenly calling; though we are in the world, we are increasingly not "of" it if we follow the upward way. Therefore, when we are born again, we are no longer in a friendly environment. We were once right at home here, but when

God's life came in, so too came feelings of alienation and separation from this world. Once we were able to think as the world thinks, lust after the things the world lusts after, find our pleasure in its pastimes. But no more.

We are chosen—but not solely for privilege. The world, misinterpreting the phrase *chosen people*, reacts with animosity. Actually, it means we have been chosen to *be* a blessing, not just to receive a blessing. God's original covenant with Abraham ("I will make of *you* a blessing") is the same mandate we receive upon our new birth. We are called to "declare the wonderful deeds of Him who called us out of darkness and into His marvelous light." The responsibility of bearing His name before the nations, of representing Him worthily, is upon us. We are chosen to serve.

The term *chosen* has two dimensions. Jesus says to His disciples in John 15:16, "You did not choose me, but I chose you," and yet we are also told, "Let him who is thirsty come" (Revelation 22:17), for God "is forbearing . . . not wishing that any should perish" (2 Peter 3:9). It is clear that the chosen become so because they are the ones who choose to answer that call.

Race refers not to ethnic heritage but is, rather, a biological term meaning kind or species. We are a new species, a phenomenon on the earth:

Instead of the thorn shall come up the cypress; instead of the brier shall come up the myrtle; and it shall be to the Lord for a memorial, for an everlasting sign which shall not be cut off.

Isaiah 55:13

In this day, Isaiah is saying, God will create a new species. Where there was brier and thorn He will bring up cypress and myrtle; what is prickly and repellent will be made lovely and fragrant; what is useless will be made evergreen and fruitful. Now, into us, where there was biological life only, tainted by greed and self-preservation, thorny with self-seeking, barren with egotism, He has transplanted eternal, divine life, imperishable in its purity, life-giving in its perfection. The promise given through Isaiah reached its time of fulfillment in the resurrection and glorification of Jesus Christ, when at last the outpouring of His Spirit could transform humanity.

WE ARE A ROYAL PRIESTHOOD

In God's sight we are kings and priests: regal by virtue of our divine heritage, priests by function. In the world to come we are destined to reign with Christ Jesus (2 Timothy 2:12; Revelation 5:10); for now, we are called to be priests. Our work in this world is first and foremost to minister to God Himself. We are ordained to praise Him (to give thanks for all that He *does*) and to worship (to consider and love Him for all that He *is*). As the Temple singers sang day and night, we too are to live constantly in a place of praise by our thoughts, words, and deeds.

A second part of our priesthood is suggested in the Latin word for priest, *pontifex*, which means "bridge-builder." We are called to represent others before the throne of God. The Levitical High Priest wore on his chest a breastplate studded with jewels, each representing one of the tribes of Israel. Upon his shoulders were two amulets, similarly engraved. This is a picture of the spiritual fact that we, like the Lord Jesus, our great and constant Intercessor, are to carry the needs of others to God in heart-felt intercession.

Thirdly, we are called to represent God to the world. The Levitical priests wore robes of blue and white, visual reminders that their God was both as omnipotent and omnipresent as the blue sky above them, and as pure and holy as the whiteness of the finest linen. We are called to declare these truths by the quality of our lives.

WE ARE A HOLY NATION

It is difficult to think of a word more distorted and misunderstood than the word *holy*. To the world, *holy* conjures up a smug, sterile, negative self-righteousness, or a chilly untested kind of virtue. The phrases *Holy Roller*, *holy Joe* or *holier-than-thou* connote sanctimonious pride and hypocrisy.

"Holy" is, in fact, a word of great richness and beauty, for it is the word by which God is chiefly described. It conveys the idea that He is absolutely real, complete, whole, one hundred percent, undefiled by sin, falsehood, or pretense, undiluted in intensity. God uses that word for Himself repeatedly throughout Scripture, and in the giving of the Law issues this command: "You shall be holy unto me; for I the Lord am holy" (Leviticus 20:26).

What God means is that we are to be *hagios*, separate, not just *from* the world, but *to* Him. If we look at the Nazirites described in Numbers 6, people who were called to live in special devotion to God, we see that they were not so much to live in negative reaction to the things of the world as they were to live in positive assimilation of the things of God. The Nazirite Samson was recognizable by his long hair as being dedicated to God rather than to current fashion. Our separation is to be evident in general holiness of lifestyle.

WE ARE GOD'S OWN POSSESSION

The King James Version of the Bible translates this passage, "God's peculiar people." The world may very well consider this an apt description of the people of God! Actually, the word *peculiar* from the Latin means "to have exclusive possession of something." It is a term applied to a slave who is private property, echoing Isaiah 43:21: "The people whom I formed *for myself* that they might declare my praise." Paul also reminds us in 1 Corinthians 6:20 that we are no longer our own. We have been bought with a price. We have been ransomed and redeemed ("bought back") so we belong now to God.

William Barclay points out that our being owned by God is what gives us our worth, just as their possession by a great

man or woman gives modest objects imputed value. The
Jeu de Paume, the lovely Parisian gallery once filled with
masterpieces by Van Gogh, Gauguin, and other post-
Impressionists, also displayed their brushes, pencils, and
trowels. These were, of course, ordinary instruments, sold
in any art supply store, but unique for what they became in
the hands of their owners. Belonging to God makes us
priceless.

OUR NEW HEARTS

So, our position is changed. We are now justified, saved,
adopted into God's family. We are kings and priests, chosen
by God, regarded by Him as holy, His very own people.

But these facts refer only to our external identities. What
about our hearts? Centuries ago, God made a staggering
promise to His people through the prophet Ezekiel:

> *A new heart I will give you, and a new spirit I will put within you;*
> *and I will take out of your flesh the heart of stone and give you a heart*
> *of flesh. And I will put my spirit within you, and cause you to walk*
> *in my statutes and be careful to observe my ordinances.*
> Ezekiel 36:26–27

What does this heart of flesh consist of? Basically, it is
God's heart, transplanted within us. In Galatians 5:22 we
find what is called the "fruit" of the Holy Spirit, that is, the
natural outpouring of that which motivates God: "Love, joy,
peace, patience, kindness, goodness, faithfulness, gentleness, self-control."

Those are not attitudes that we try to display, for that
would make them works. They are intended to be the natural
manifestation (fruit) of His life within. Neither are they
commodities. ("I need more patience, Lord.") F. B. Meyer
counsels us to remember that Galatians 5:22 is the description
of a Person who now lives inside us, and pray instead,
"Lord, let me live today more yielded to You, letting Your
infinite reservoir of love and peace (etc.) be my supply."

Another description of the new heart within is the famous and beloved passage, 1 Corinthians 13. The key to understanding this Scripture is to recognize that "Love" is a Person, the Spirit of Jesus Christ. Therefore, the *Person* within us is patient and kind; He is not jealous or boastful; He is not arrogant or rude. He doesn't insist on His own way; He is not irritable or resentful; He doesn't rejoice at wrong, but rejoices in the right. He bears all things, believes all things, hopes all things, endures all things. He never fails.

Our fullest picture, of course, is given in the Gospels, for these are the accounts of how Love looked in everyday life, how He poured Himself out in an unending stream of healing and teaching and delivering those around Him. They make up our portrait of the Lord Jesus Christ.

RECEIVING THE NEW HEART

How do we receive this new heart and character? By girding our loins and imitating Jesus? Imitation, in Thomas Merton's phrase, "can degenerate into mere impersonation, if it remains only exterior."[2] Imitation without the fuel to carry it off leads to frustration and despair. In Ephesians 4:22–24 we are told:

> *Put off your old nature which belongs to your former manner of life and is corrupt through deceitful lusts, and be renewed in the spirit of your minds, and put on the new nature, created after the likeness of God in true righteousness and holiness.*

Expressed another way, we receive our new hearts by renouncing our old ways, beholding our Lord, and walking in His ways.

RENOUNCING THE OLD

Renunciation is a relatively simple thing to understand, if not to do. Romans 13:12–14 challenges:

Let us then cast off the works of darkness and put on the armor of light; let us conduct ourselves becomingly as in the day, not in reveling and drunkenness, not in debauchery and licentiousness, not in quarreling and jealousy. But put on the Lord Jesus Christ, and make no provision for the flesh, to gratify its desires.

The death of Christ has freed us not only from the power of death, but of sin as well. We are no longer compelled to sin, but are free to choose to walk where we will. As temptations continue to come (or even to intensify) the Holy Spirit will set off a warning; when our old natures raise their ugly heads, the light of the Spirit within will expose them, and we can refuse to yield to their pressures. In fact, as the Bible puts it, we now have the power to cast off our old works as we would shed filthy clothes.

BEHOLDING THE NEW

At the same time we are putting off the old, we are called to put on the new. Romans 12:2 gives us the key:

Do not be conformed to this world but be transformed by the renewal of your mind, that you may prove what is the will of God, what is good and acceptable and perfect.

How is this renewal accomplished? In his second letter to the Corinthians Paul answers this question by recalling the dynamics of Moses' relationship with Yahweh. When Moses came down from Mount Sinai, with the two tables of the testimony in his hand, he did not know that the skin of his face shone because he had been talking with God. Like Moses, as we behold "the glory of the Lord," we, too, will be changed into His likeness "from one degree of glory to another" (2 Corinthians 3:18).

Thomas A. Smail explains Paul's analogy, noting that the Greek word for *beholding* can be translated both "contemplating" and "reflecting," as in a mirror: "As the believer looks to Christ and opens himself to him, the knowledge of Christ that he gains is never simply objective and intellectual knowledge, it is knowledge that begins to change him, so that he begins to reflect that to which he has been exposed, and its likeness begins to be formed in him."[3]

How do we behold? The same way Moses did: by spending time with the Lord, receiving the Word of God, and talking with God. In other words, we absorb the Lord's character by soaking up His Word (in Bible study and meditation), by talking with Him in prayer, and by learning to live in awareness of His presence.

David speaks of the latter in Psalm 27:8: "Thy face, Lord, do I seek." We are called to do the same—to seek Him in all things, in people, in the circumstances of our day, in providence, in revelation, and in the promptings of our hearts. David also knew that the secret to achieving purity of heart was by hiding God's Word there (Psalm 119:11). Jesus confirmed it: "If you abide in me, and my words abide in you, ask whatever you will, and it shall be done for you" (John 15:7). He knew that if our minds are soaked, steeped in, continuously beholding His Word, then our will and our desires will be in tune with His will. Our prayers will naturally be ones that He can readily answer.

As we prayerfully, diligently feed on His Word we will take on and reflect His mind, and the fuel for walking in His ways will be steady and unfailing.

WALK IN THE LIGHT

Finally, we must walk in obedience to our new hearts and our renewed minds, for the blessing of knowing only comes in the doing. When Scripture exhorts us to "put on" the character of Christ this is not a command to be hypocritical (as it would be if there were no internal goodness as foundation); it is a direction of how to prime the pump, so to speak. F. B. Meyer says, "First we reflect . . . then we shall be changed. If you try to represent Jesus in your character

and behaviour, you will become transfigured into his likeness. Love makes like. Imitation produces assimilation."[4] We
are told to act as if the godly characteristics we long for are
actually there.

In the days of King David, the chief of his army, Joab,
encouraged his men with these words: "Be of good courage,
and let us *play* the man for our people, and for the cities of
our God; and may the Lord do what seems good to him" (2
Samuel 10:12). That phrase, *play the man*, means "pretend to
be brave," but the promise is implicit: And you *will* be brave.
It is not a trick of mind over matter; it is the Kingdom method
of believing before seeing, *so as to see*.

As we walk steadily onward, believing that the character of
God is actually growing within us, we can act as if it were so,
and will one day find that it is so. If we act as if we were kind,
loving, joyful, and peaceful, and we are taking in and doing
God's Word, we will be those things.

It may not take place overnight. As Eugene Peterson has
remarked in his book of the same title, what counts is "a long
obedience in the same direction." The Syrian captain Naaman, strong and blessed in all ways, was, unfortunately, a
leper. Going to the prophet Elijah for help, he expected
elaborate instructions on how to be healed. The message is
humbling to the point of being infuriating to the proud
soldier. He is to bathe seven times in the modest little Jordan,
a river he feels is not even fit to be compared to the great
rivers of his native land. And yet, as Naaman obeyed, day
after day, seven times, "his flesh was restored like the flesh
of a little child" (2 Kings 5:14).

At his coronation, Octavius, the first of the Roman emper-
ors, took the name Augustus to mark his new, august status.
As we consider and receive our new, most exalted position as
sons and daughters of God, new creatures positionally and
actually, let us take on the name above all names—the name
of Jesus Christ—and show forth the family resemblance.

5

THE GIVING OF
YOUR "FIRST" NAME

To him who conquers I will give some of the hidden manna, and I will give him a white stone, with a new name written on the stone which no one knows except him who receives it.　　　　Revelation 2:17

We have already considered our collective identity in Christ—our "family" name. We are a nation of kings and priests, holy and chosen, reconciled, adopted, and embraced by the Father. We have a new position in the eyes of the Father because we are in Christ and Christ is in us. Positionally we have been given the "white stone," the ancient sign for acquittal. Manna we recognize as God's miraculous provision to the Israelites when they were in the desert, far from a supply of wheat for bread. Our manna is the Lord Himself, the Bread of Life, supplying our energy through His Word and His Spirit dwelling within us. We have learned that, like the Israelites, we must gather manna each day, abiding in the Word and in Him.

But in addition to our "family" name, we also have a

"first" name, one that belongs to each of us privately. It is our "new name," which no one knows except him who receives it. The *Interpreter's Bible* comments, "There is a central citadel in each personality which only God shares. The new name represents the individual personality achieved only through the grace of Christ. The believer is a new man; but he is not a new man just like every other new man. He is eternally something individual and different and eternally prized by God."[1]

William Barclay confirms the idea of uniqueness by showing that there are two Greek words for *new*: *neos*, which means new in terms of time, but which says nothing of singularity (many hundreds of thousands of cars may be "new," but they are mass-produced, and therefore identical in design and function). The word used in Revelation, however, *kainos*, speaks of newness of quality; nothing like it has ever been made before. The "new" Jerusalem, the "new" song of heaven, even the "new" heavens themselves all refer to things never seen before. This "new name," then, speaks of a unique character and destiny that God alone knows and will reveal only to the person He intends to possess it.

Though all believers are called to be kind, to be filled with love, and though we are all regarded as children of the Most High God, and we are all to keep a lively sense of our corporate identity as members of the Body of Christ, we must at the same time recognize that we are individuals, precisely designed, irreplaceable, and precious to our Creator.

WHAT IS A NAME?

Which brings us then to the definition of our mystic names: Our names are the unique character and mission by which God knows us.

We are not always talking here of literal names (though God will on occasion give us a literal new name). I was speaking on this theme at a young persons' retreat. A civil engineer named Tom asked, with mock seriousness, "You mean in my prayer time the Lord might start calling me Ralph?" We all laughed and I explained again how we weren't talking of literal new names here, but rather what a name represents: character and mission.

I shared this story later with another group and afterward a lady came to me with an interesting story. In her prayer time, the Lord *had* actually given a new name to her, a Hebrew word, "Rahah." When she looked it up in a lexicon she discovered it meant fear, which she took at first to mean godly fear—as in the fear of the Lord. Grateful for receiving it, she even had it engraved on a ring her husband had bought her in Israel.

As it turned out, the word had a different significance. A few years later, a Jewish believer in Jesus, upon hearing the story, expressed an uneasiness. "Are you sure that is your name?" he asked. "It just doesn't seem to me that the Lord would name someone 'Fear.' " Troubled by his question, she had stopped wearing the ring. Now, she said, she was confused over what it was all about.

I felt led to ask her if she had ever been troubled by fears in the past. Confirming this, she added that it seemed her family had always been prone to fear, and that she'd had a lot of prayer for the healing of this inherited tendency.

"Then perhaps God was revealing your old name to you," I suggested, "just as He did to Jacob. Sometimes we need to see and acknowledge our deepest needs before He can heal and change us."

As we ended our conversation, she sounded relieved, knowing that the Lord was already at work in her to bring her into her new identity in Him. Later I remembered a similar transformation in Hannah Hurnard's classic book, *Hinds' Feet on High Places*. The heroine, Much Afraid, after a great struggle makes the decision to leave her relatives, the Craven Fearings, and venture into a new kingdom with the Shepherd. At the end of her journeys she discovers that her new name is Grace and Glory.

HOW DOES GOD DISCLOSE OUR NAMES?

As we have seen, God does call. But too many believers miss the fullness of their individual calling. They dissipate their energies because they don't know how to focus on the call upon their lives. Perhaps it is because they do not recognize the ways God has of conveying to them their new names. Let's examine a few of the infinite varieties of ways the Lord has of disclosing our new names to us.

OUR OWN NAMES

Most names mean something, and even when they appear to have been given to us quite casually they can be used by God to reveal truth to us about ourselves; a clue to our future identities and life's work can sometimes be found in the names we already have.

This is mysterious, but it is scriptural. Moses, bearing an Egyptian name given him by his adoptive mother, could have seen in its Hebrew equivalent Moshe (to draw out) both his origin (drawn from the waters of the Nile) and his destiny (to draw God's people out of their slavery in Egypt).

A believing friend, Pamela, who struggles with a pessimistic nature, was encouraged when she learned that her name meant "honey." Filled with a special love for God's Word, she delights in the many comparisons to honey of the sweetness of God's Word, such as in Psalm 19:10: "Sweeter also than honey and drippings of the honeycomb."

Ruth battles what she once condemned in herself as hypersensitivity, being too thin-skinned and morose. Looking up her name one day in a dictionary, she learned that her name meant "pity." God showed her that her pain over the sufferings of others was not morbidity, but a genuine reflection of His own compassionate heart toward His people. It also served to confirm her in her ministry of inner healing and restoration.

Deborah finds her name ironic. Named by her great-grandmother for the Old Testament judge who rallied the Israelites to fight for their Promised Land, Deborah recognizes in herself a tendency to be judgmental of those who are not so zealous as she for the things of the Lord. However, she also looks to her name as a promise that God will temper her enthusiasm with understanding, so that she is properly equipped to lead in a godly way.

Tom was a modern-day "doubting Thomas," by nature and by his Jesuitical education that taught him to question everything. He met Jesus Christ when he was miraculously healed of Hodgkin's disease. Now he uses his natural skepticism as equipment to minister to others who have trouble believing before they see.

ADMIRATION OF CERTAIN TRAITS

Yearnings for a particular character trait can be a clue to what God intends us to be, if we will but ask for these qualities. We might call this the Wizard-of-Oz syndrome, for the Cowardly Lion, the Straw Man, and the others looking for courage or intelligence personify the longing in every human for what he or she lacks. Since we receive by asking, and God knows our need *before* we ask, can we not see these promptings as originating with Him?

My husband resisted the Lord for a year or so after my conversion. When he was finally a believer I asked him just what change in my life had convinced him that God was real. (Secretly, I hoped he would praise my serenity, my goodness, the general sterling example I had set in those intervening months.) Instead, he thought for a moment and then grinned: "Your sarcasm was less strident."

A humbling observation. But it showed how far I had come in my aspirations, at least, since I had begun to walk with the Lord. Years of dorm life, the free speech movement, and my own proclivity for words had made my tongue a ready weapon. I had always counted on their power for defensive and offensive purposes. But when Jesus Christ came to dwell inside me, as Graham Kerr once put it, "My powers of exaggeration were greatly diminished," my sarcasm was blunted, and kindness and gentleness took on a new appeal.

I remember one day reading the thirty-first chapter of Proverbs about the "excellent wife," and I ran headlong into these words: "The teaching of kindness is on her tongue." I felt a pang of yearning in my soul for such a quality. As I prayed and meditated on this idea, I came to see that kind words, spoken in the Spirit, contained far more power than my former "wit" or "eloquence," such as it was. It became my prayer that my desire for this quality was a prelude to God's actually working it into my character, making it part of my new name . . . my identity.

We may yearn for the courage of the martyred Stephen, the generosity of Barnabas, the obedience of the virgin Mary, the boldness of Daniel, the loyalty of John the Baptist, recognizing our weaknesses in contrast to their strengths. Paradoxically, it is in these very areas of weakness where God can work His greatest miracles. Jacob's sons Levi and Simeon led their brothers in a vicious vendetta against the Prince of Shechem for seducing their sister, Dinah, even though the Prince loved and planned to marry her. For this murderous anger, Levi forfeited his seniority in the line for his father's blessing (Genesis 49:5–7). By the time of the Exodus, however, the Levites' anger had been tempered into godly zeal, and it was this zeal by which they "ordained themselves," in God's words, as His first priests (Exodus 32:25–29). God had transformed their ancestors' weakness into a strength.

So, too, He can change our cowardice, our sarcasm, our stinginess, our laziness, into the very traits we long to have. David Brainerd, eighteenth-century missionary to the Delaware Indians, was grieved by the coldness he found in his heart, his comparative apathy toward the people he was called to minister to. As he cried out to God in prayer for love for them, God set his heart on fire and turned him into a legend among soulwinners.

THE ENCOURAGEMENT OF FAMILY AND FRIENDS

Just as our husbands or wives sometimes have a much truer view of our characters than we do, so do our friends. We can, therefore, learn much about our new names by listening to their observations. It took Barnabas, at God's direction, to talk Paul into resuming ministry after a time of self-imposed exile. Jonathan, at the risk of his own life, did God's work of affirming the future king, his friend David. God may give us glimpses of what He intends to do in a close friend, or our spouse. Through them the Lord may also give us a clue as to where our ministries might lie.

If friends regularly ask our advice or comment on our "wisdom," we shouldn't shake it off as just flattery, but consider the possibility that the Lord has prompted them to say it for our encouragement. If we are sought out to intercede for others and we hear comments like, "I knew I could talk to you," let us acknowledge that the Lord is shining forth from us, and be grateful for our usefulness in this way. When things need to be organized and our phones start ringing, we may need to accept the idea that God has given us special skills and humbly receive the mantle of leadership.

It is ironic that many of us don't realize our strongest gifts. The man with the beautiful singing voice, the woman with the ability to listen to all points of view and then synthesize them articulately—they may not even realize that these things are gifts at all. My husband and I are constantly after one of our close friends to "be funny," for he has a wonderful way of turning ordinary, even painful, incidents into stories that make us weep with laughter. But we have had to quote Proverbs 17:22: "A merry heart doeth good like a medicine," (kjv) to make him realize that his is a gift that greatly ministers to us!

A Marriage Encounter weekend we attended some years ago began with people being asked to introduce themselves and to name the one trait that attracted them most to their future spouses. It was almost funny to hear some of the answers. A man said of his dumpy middle-aged wife: "Her beauty." Another woman remarked of her stern-looking husband: "His terrific sense of humor." I realized later that these were the answers of people looking through the eyes of love, the kind of love that caused Jesus to look at Simon and call him Peter, or see in Jacob an Israel. Perhaps what we fall in love with is a momentary God-given glimpse of what He desires to bring forth in that person.

A NEW NAME CAN IDENTIFY MISSION

In the book of Nehemiah a remnant of God's people who have come back from exile undertake the restoration of the city of Jerusalem. Under Nehemiah's direction, each family is placed at a precise point on the wall and is assigned a task, building or defending other builders from their enemies. In addition to telling us our new names in terms of character, God also wishes to show us our "place on the wall," our mission, so that we won't waste our time or our gifts duplicating the effort of the person next to us. For our fulfillment and for the work of the Kingdom we must seek to hear His directions. Here are some ways through which He directs us to our missions.

THROUGH THE WORD OF THE LORD

The prophets of old announced, "The word of the Lord came unto me," and so we too can learn to let His Word come to us. Jesus, returning to the synagogue in Nazareth where He had grown up, chose to read the passage from Isaiah with which He identified Himself and His mission (Luke 4:18). John the Baptist recognized his mission from one of Isaiah's prophecies as well: "I am the voice of one crying in the wilderness," he quoted when asked if he were the Christ (John 1:23). So we, too, can begin to learn part of our identity and mission from the Word of God, by waiting upon His *rhema* (a Scripture especially applicable to us).

As I began to study the Bible in earnest, my heart yearned to share its treasures with others, but I hadn't really ever had the courage to admit that wish, even to myself. It seemed much too lofty an ambition.

One day, I came to the book of Ezra, a record of the Israelites' return from Babylon. Ezra was identified as a scribe skilled in the law of Moses. Then my eyes fell on Ezra 7:10: "For Ezra had set his heart to study the law of the Lord, and to do it, and to teach his statutes and ordinances in Israel." Suddenly I understood that cryptic phrase "the Lord quickened His Word." Those words seemed written in neon, written just for me, so perfectly did they sum up the longing of my heart. It was as if the Lord had handed me a written invitation to teach His Word.

But was I being presumptuous? How could I possibly even think about teaching from this fathomless Book? I had never taught anything but worldly literature. Wouldn't I have to go to seminary? Start my education all over?

I continued reading. The following verses (11–20) were a letter from King Artaxerxes authorizing Ezra to lead his people back to Jerusalem. I read verse 19: "The vessels that have been given you for the service of the house of your God, you shall deliver before the God of Jerusalem." It was a mandate to use the "vessels" He had given me—the mind, the skills, the worldly experience in teaching—to serve the Kingdom; I was now accountable to God for the way I used them.

I pondered this. One last question remained: Where and how was I to be prepared for this? Where would I find answers for the hungry people I hoped to help? How inadequate I was!

The Lord answered in the next verse, almost as if He had anticipated our having this very conversation: "And whatever else is required for the house of your God, which you have occasion to provide, you may provide it out of the

king's treasury." My inadequacy was not a factor here.
Whatever I was called on to provide, I would have out of "the
king's treasury" of wisdom. If I would simply be a vessel and
study diligently what He provided for me, He would be my
source of supply.

THROUGH DREAMS

In Genesis 37:5–11 the boy Joseph, beloved by his father
and consequently hated by his eleven jealous brothers, made
matters worse when he told them of two dreams he had had.
In the first, the family was binding sheaves in the field.
Joseph's sheaf stood upright while the others' sheaves bowed
down to it. In the second, the sun, the moon, and eleven
stars were bowing down to him. This dream alienated even
Joseph's father, who recognized himself and Joseph's mother
as the sun and the moon, and he rebuked the young man for
his arrogance.

Yet these prophetic dreams of leadership were fulfilled.
After being sold into slavery in Egypt, Joseph ultimately
found himself given favor because of his God-given revelations and wisdom, eventually becoming second in power
only to the Pharaoh. In the intervening years of unjust
imprisonment and what seemed like abandonment, how
tightly Joseph must have clung to the identity God had
promised him in those early boyhood dreams.

Jackie Pullinger, British missionary to the drug addicts of
the walled city, Hong Kong, writes in her book *Chasing the
Dragon* that as a little girl she had met "a proper missionary"
in Sunday school and had thereafter "had a dim picture of
myself sitting at the door of a mud hut, a sort of White Queen
in Africa, feeling worthy."[2] Several years later, as a committed Christian, she dreamed that she and her family were
looking at a map of Africa. To her surprise in the middle was
a pink country labeled "Hong Kong." Hong Kong, of course,
is not in Africa and it was a British Crown colony, not a

country. What could the dream mean? It was as if the very incongruity served to emphasize the name *Hong Kong*.

Later through a prophecy the Lord promised to instruct and guide her: "Go . . . trust Me, and I will lead you." Upon her pastor's advice she set out as Abraham had, not really knowing where she was headed. As Gladys Aylward had journeyed in faith to China, so Jackie used all her money to purchase passage on a ship bound for the Orient.

After several weeks of travel she looked out upon Hong Kong. "The sight took my breath away. All the places we had passed by earlier on the voyage seemed so flat by comparison. . . . I found myself filled with peace and as I recognized that this was the place God had chosen, I said thank you." God, who has promised that He will give wisdom liberally, had brought her to the meeting place of a dream and reality.

THROUGH VISIONS

We may be accustomed to thinking that only Old Testament prophets had visions, and yet Joel 2:28, speaking of the day of the outpouring of God's Spirit, promises that "your sons and your daughters shall prophesy, your old men shall dream dreams, and your young men shall see visions." As we have seen, the apostle Peter had a vision that replaced his parochialism with a new godly outlook. In Acts 10:11–13 it is recorded that Peter "saw the heaven opened, and something descending, like a great sheet, let down by four corners upon the earth. In it were all kinds of animals and reptiles and birds of the air. And there came a voice to him, 'Rise, Peter; kill and eat.' " Peter's reply, "No, Lord!" came almost involuntarily from the depths of a Jewish heart, raised since childhood on the notion of its exclusive status as God's people. For God to pronounce His ancient taboos obsolete, telling Peter to take the Gospel to the despised Gentiles, toppled the entire universe and turned him personally inside out. Yet Peter obeyed and came more in line with God's perspective.

Paul's ministry was similarly changed and widened by his vision of a Macedonian man calling out his people's need to hear the gospel.

David Wilkerson, a self-styled "skinny preacher" from rural Pennsylvania, was haunted by a modern-day "vision"—a photograph in *Life* magazine of New York gang members on trial for murder. Against all logic, following only the ache of his heart for these lost young men, Wilkerson answered God's call to go and minister to them on the streets. His book *The Cross and the Switchblade* records his personal transformation, as through him the Lord established Teen Challenge, now a worldwide ministry to drug addicts.

What finally gave me the courage to begin to teach God's Word was a momentary flash of a vision. As I worshiped with friends, several of whom were Catholic, I began to see that though we were all relatively new believers, many of them had never before even owned a Bible. I at least had had years of Bible teaching in the form of Sunday school stories and hymn lyrics. One day it seemed as if I were in the middle of a nest of tiny baby robins, their almost transparent necks stretched taut, their mouths wide with hunger, cheeping for food. Whatever little I knew was more than they had; and I recognized this as a signal to begin where I saw the need.

Corrie ten Boom, a Dutch Christian, and her sister Betsie, were imprisoned by the Nazis for helping the Jews during World War II. One day in their prayer time the Lord asked them what they were going to do in the years after the war. Betsie felt that they were to open a large house where concentration camp survivors could come until they felt ready to live again in the outside world. She would speak in detail of a beautiful house with inlaid floors, a broad, sweeping staircase, statues set in the walls, and gardens where the people could plant bright flowers.

Though her sister died, Corrie was miraculously released and spent the next year speaking to groups throughout Holland, telling them of God's love and provision to them in the midst of their trials, and sharing Betsie's vision for the

war victims. At such a meeting a lady came forward to tell
Corrie that the Lord had directed her to give her home for
this work, and she invited Corrie to come and see it. Corrie
tells of the trip in her book *The Hiding Place*. As they
approached the house, Corrie asked:

"Are there—" my throat was dry. "Are there inlaid
wood floors inside, and a broad gallery around the
central hall, and bas-relief statues set along the walls?"
    Mrs. Bierens de Haan looked at me in surprise.
"You've been here and I don't recall—"
    "No," I said, "I heard about it from—"
    I stopped. How could I explain what I did not
understand?
    "From someone who's been here," she finished sim-
ply, not understanding my perplexity.
    "Yes," I said. "From someone who's been here."[3]

THROUGH THE MOTIVATIONAL GIFTS

In Romans 12:6 we are exhorted: "Having gifts that differ
according to the grace given to us, let us use them: if
prophecy, in proportion to our faith; if service, in our
serving; he who teaches, in his teaching; he who exhorts, in
his exhortation, he who contributes, in liberality; he who
gives aid, with zeal; he who does acts of mercy, with
cheerfulness." Today there are many teachings available to
the Church about how to recognize our basic motivations,
offering such examples as John the Baptist, the prototype for
the prophetic motivation, or Barnabas, the exhorter, or Paul,
the teacher. These studies show the range of concerns and
ways of looking at situations that exist within the Body of
Christ. They also address the ways one person's concerns
can be misunderstood by others who are coming to a
situation from other angles.
    In our "cell group" (a weekly church group of twelve
members, gathered for fellowship and prayer) we took the

time to study these ministries and motivations and found out why we often see things in such diverse ways. After discussion (and much laughter) we came away with a greater appreciation not only for each other's contributions but with an appreciation and a sense of validation for ourselves as well.

My husband, prophetic by nature, had suffered misunderstanding from many people (not the least of which me) because they couldn't understand his "gloomy" assessment of things. I myself am an exhorter, or encourager, who constantly looks for solutions to problems ("What's salvageable here?"), while the prophet focuses on the problem itself and often defines it in stark and even confrontative terms. Before we realized that each had a legitimate, God-given point of view, we often stymied each other and doubted our own gifts. ("Am I just being critical?" Michael would ask; "Am I being a Pollyanna?" I would worry.) When we learned to understand the other's viewpoint, we realized that together we were equipped to handle most problems.

We also learned to appreciate others in our group. So-and-so's "hypersensitivity" we learned is actually motivated by mercy; another, whom we have judged as "unspiritual" and "nit-picking" because of what we thought was an undue concern for practicalities, we learned has a gift of service. Another's preoccupation with the exact wording of a quote from Scripture is not a deliberate effort to be tiresome; his motivational gift is teaching, and his concern for accuracy is God-given.

Teachings on motivational gifts stress that these categories are not to be used as cop-outs for narrow mindedness or refusal to change and grow, for we must listen hard (and together) to receive the whole counsel of God on a matter. What we do learn is that by God's grace His servants' motivations are varied and complementary, and that in the Kingdom there is room for everyone. As Paul writes in 1 Corinthians 12:4–6: "There are varieties of gifts, but the same Spirit; and there are varieties of service, but the same Lord;

and there are varieties of working, but it is the same God who inspires them all in every one."

THROUGH OPPORTUNITIES FOR SERVICE

The thrust of circumstances, combined with the opening of our eyes to a particular need, is often God's way of bringing forth from us those gifts and ministries He has placed within. He brings them into full bloom in service to others, nurturing in us certain character traits along the way. A good example is found in the story of David (1 Kings 17). Sent by his father to take food to his older brothers fighting in Saul's army, he hears the Philistine giant Goliath blaspheming Yahweh and insulting the Israelites because they have sent no one out to fight him. David is incensed that no one has avenged the name of God, and in anger and faith he volunteers. In the midst of derision he fells the giant with one well-placed blow from his slingshot and launches himself on the road that will make him the greatest king in Israel's history.

The need was also the call for Mother Teresa, already a teaching nun at a convent school in Calcutta. Malcolm Muggeridge in *Something Beautiful for God* writes, "She had occasion to go into some of the very poorest streets of Calcutta . . . and suddenly realized that she belonged there, not in her Loreto convent with its pleasant garden, eager schoolgirls, congenial colleagues and rewarding work. It was, as she put it, 'a call within a call.' "[4] Since that time she has ministered to the dying poor as though they were Jesus Christ Himself, inspiring the world by her work and example.

As a young medical missionary in India, Dr. Paul Brand, a world-renowned orthopedic surgeon at Carville, Louisiana, Leprosy Hospital, visited a leprosy sanitarium. As a hand surgeon he was puzzled as to why the disease should damage hands and feet but there was no one who could answer; perhaps because of fear of contagion, no orthopedic surgeon had ever worked with lepers.

Seeing a man struggle to put on his sandal, Dr. Brand

asked him to squeeze his hand. Expecting a weak grip, he was startled at the man's great strength.

> That was the clue. Somewhere in that severely deformed hand were powerfully good muscles. . . . Could they be freed?
>
> I felt a tingling as if the whole universe was revolving around me. I knew I had arrived in my place.
>
> That single incident in 1947 changed my life. . . . Every detail of that scene—the people standing around the grounds, the shade of the tree, the questioning face of the patient whose hand I was holding—is still etched into my mind. It was my moment, and I had felt a call of the Spirit of God.[5]

We should, however, heed the warning of the Quaker Thomas Kelly who wrote, "We cannot die on every cross." We need to focus only on the tasks that God has given us and to do them in His way; the need is not always the call, for we may not be the ones whom God has assigned to the task, or we may not yet have the maturity to do it God's way.

Moses saw clearly the need of his enslaved people, but when he tried in his own way to remedy their internecine quarrels, he found himself reviled by the very people he was trying to help. Worse yet, in trying to protect his brothers from the Egyptians, he committed murder and had to flee to the desert, an exile. It was forty years before God could send him back to deliver His people in His way.

Recognition of need should be accompanied by an inner witness, a peace, a sense of rightness, the feeling, "at last, this is my place," as Paul Brand expressed it. Jim Elliot, the martyred missionary to the Auca Indians of Ecuador, wrote of this inner witness as he embarked for his work in 1952:

> All the thrill of boyhood dreams came on me just now outside, watching the sky die in the sea on every side. . . . Now I am actually at sea—a passenger, of course, but at sea nevertheless—and bound for Ecuador.

Strange—or is it?—that childish hopes should be answered in the will of God for this now? . . . Joy, sheer joy, and thanksgiving fill and encompass me. . . . God has done and is doing all I ever desired, much more than I ever asked. Praise, praise to the God of Heaven, and to His Son Jesus. . . .[6]

We may never experience the near-ecstasy of some, but we can rely on the Holy Spirit within us to reign in our hearts and let us know when we are in the center of the will of God (Colossians 3:15). If we take note of those activities and times when we feel energized, refreshed even after hard work, and joyful in the task—("I delight to do thy will, O my God" Psalm 40:8)—we will find the work God has for us.

THROUGH OUR NATURAL SKILLS AND TRAINING

It is not always God's will that we radically change direction in our lives as we follow Him. C. S. Lewis once wrote of Christianity: "That's a school where they can always use your previous work, whatever subject it was on." What *does* change is our motivation.

When Jesus called the group of Galilean fishermen, He called them to become fishers of men: to change not their skills but their goal. As apostles, they did, in fact, forsake their livelihood to go and preach. Many of us will simply continue on the road we started upon with the gifts we have already discovered; only now we will be using them to the glory of our Father, rather than solely for our self-fulfillment.

In these cases we can take our calling and direction from the talents and skills we already have. In Exodus 35:25 it is recorded that in making the elaborate and beautiful curtains and hangings for the first Tabernacle, "All women who had ability spun with their hands and brought what they had spun in blue and purple and scarlet stuff and fine twined linen; all the women *whose hearts were moved with ability* spun the goats' hair. . . ." The very skill they possessed *was* the

call of God upon them, and they came gladly to offer their
craftsmanship to Him for His work.

Sometimes even unpleasant experiences or training sessions when redeemed can point to our place of service in the
Kingdom. When Joseph, after years as a slave and a prisoner,
finally by God's providence became prime minister of Egypt,
his years of administrative training enabled him to save
millions from starvation. He then could see that his brothers'
treachery in selling him into slavery and his subsequent
mistreatment were all part of God's equipping him for
service. "You meant evil against me," he told his remorseful
brothers, "but God meant it for good" (Genesis 50:20).

Moses was raised by the very Pharaoh who had decreed
his death. In that royal court he received the best education
the ancient world had to offer (arts, mathematics, military
strategy, engineering). When he became God's man to
deliver His people, he was equipped. Similarly, it is written
of the people of Israel that the Egyptians gave them "going-
away" gifts of silver and gold—resources they later were
used to build God's Tabernacle. The things of the world were
sanctified for use in the Kingdom (Exodus 11:2–3).

THROUGH OPPORTUNITIES AROUND US

There are many whom God calls to stay where we are. In
Mark 5:18–19 a man delivered from demons begged to join
Jesus as a disciple. But the Lord told him, "Go home to your
friends and tell them how much the Lord has done for
you. . . ." One problem exists for those of us who are called
to stay where we are. We may have a dualistic view of service
to God. That is, we think of some task, such as teaching
Sunday school or praying, as "spiritual," while a job such as
ironing clothes is "secular," and doesn't count for anything
in eternity.

God makes a point of blasting that viewpoint away. In
Zechariah 14:20 he prophesies: "On that day [when the
kingdom is established] there shall be inscribed on the bells

of the horses, Holy to the Lord. And the pots in the house of the Lord shall be as the bowls before the altar; and *every pot* in Jerusalem and Judah shall be sacred to the Lord of hosts. . . ." What once had been inscribed only on the golden coronet of God's High Priest would now signify the Lord's ownership of a humble animal of burden. And every container would be sacred to the use of the Lord.

On a retreat I met a beautiful young woman whose name, Joy, matched her countenance. As we spoke between sessions over coffee, I asked what she did in the "real world." She answered that she sold children's shoes at Bloomingdale's. I smiled sympathetically, expecting her to shake her head at the stress of such a job. But she continued without a trace of irony: "I love that job so much. When I'm kneeling in front of those kids I just feel Jesus kneeling beside me, washing their feet. I wouldn't trade it for anything in the world." What a gift, I thought, to see what some would dismiss as drudgery as a sacramental act. I remembered Paul's exhortation: "Whatever you do, do to the glory of God . . ." (1 Corinthians 10:31).

Our friend Bruce is an interior designer for a major national corporation. Like many Christian artists he went through a time of wondering whether the creation of beautiful but not specifically "religious" things was acceptable to God. Then the Lord showed him a passage in Exodus:

> *"See, the Lord has called by name Bezalel the son of Uri, son of Hur, of the tribe of Judah; and he has filled him with the Spirit of God, with ability, with intelligence, with knowledge, and with all craftsmanship, to devise artistic designs, to work in gold and silver and bronze, in cutting stones for setting, and in carving wood, for work in every skilled craft."* Exodus 35:30–33

Bruce is beginning to realize that the creation of a beautiful hotel or restaurant, if it is dedicated to the Lord, is a blessing on the earth—and that whatever is *done* for the glory of God *counts* to His glory, eternally.

My friend Suzanne found the Lord insisting that her artistic gifts be put to use. Several years ago she asked Him in prayer, "Who am I and what is my ministry?" His answer was clear: "Paint." But she saw no spiritual value in that, no way "to really reach out for Christ," as she puts it. "Though I did continue to paint, I kept seeking 'God's will' for me, thinking there must be something more spiritual for me to do."

She took on many Christian commitments, wondering why she felt little joy in them—sometimes even resenting the people she had committed herself to serve. Through this struggle she found many areas of her life that needed healing such as a tendency toward perfectionism and an actual fear of the lonely hours that painting might require. But as the Lord dealt with these things through His Word and through the counsel and prayer of other believers, she began to lay aside the "ministries" she had crammed her life with.

Soon, art workshops that she had tried unsuccessfully to get into suddenly had openings; friends, out of the blue, called to ask about her painting. Then one day, she picked up J. I. Packer's book *Keep in Step with the Spirit* and read: "There can be too much emphasis on God's habit of giving gifts that correspond to nothing that you can seem capable of doing before conversion (and God does practice this), but this idea blinds some people to the fact that the most significant gifts in the church's life are ordinary natural abilities which He sanctifies."[7] Today Suzanne is very happily painting and exhibiting her work, proclaiming God's glory in her watercolors of animals and landscapes. She now loves those hours "alone," for they are precious times to be together with the Lord as she functions in her true gift.

A used-car company in the Washington, D.C., area has as its motto: "Selling autos is our business; sharing Christ is our life." We can sell shoes, teach physics, illustrate children's books, build buildings, sew tents, plow fields, and/or wash dishes to the glory of God as long as He has called us to do it. In the doing, we may "find" ourselves, as the world puts it, in our own backyards. As we listen for our individual names, let us remember that our God is a God of infinite variety and creativity, and that what He has designed us to be and do can be done by no other.

George MacDonald, the nineteenth-century writer and mystic, has written about our new names:

Not only then has each man his individual relation to God, but each man has his peculiar relation to God. He is to God a peculiar being, made after his own fashion, and that of no one else. . . . There is a chamber also (O God, humble and accept my speech)—a chamber in God Himself, into which none can enter but the one, the individual, the peculiar man—out of which chamber that man has to bring revelation and strength for his brethren. This is that for which he was made—to reveal the secret things of the Father.[8]

6

OBSTACLES TO RECEIVING YOUR NAME

Over the door to the library at Harvard University is inscribed: "And ye shall know the truth, and the truth shall make you free" (John 8:32, KJV). For many years, my uncle told me he thought that that quotation referred to factual knowledge, and he along with millions of others searched for truth in such libraries. It was not until he entered into a personal relationship with Jesus Christ that he realized that the truth Jesus was referring to was not worldly wisdom at all. His truth is that He is Lord, that He has paid for the salvation of all human beings, and that our ceaseless search for immortality ends only in Him.

These are the foundations; but there are, as we have seen, many additional truths—truths about how God loves us and cherishes us and finds us unique and indispensable to

Himself. These truths should be setting us free from old identities and shaping our new selves. But in many lives they seem to have little effect.

"What is stopping your Word?" I asked the Lord, and His answer came in a peculiarly twentieth-century parable. One spring day I was admiring a neighbor's lush, green lawn. I asked how she and her husband, a busy doctor, found the time to keep it so beautiful.

"Oh, we don't," she laughed, telling me the name of a local lawn service. "We've really been pleased with them," she continued, "but I just got their estimate for thatching, and it was horrendous!"

Thatching? We were new homeowners and the term was just another in the arcane terminology of the suburbs. "What is that?" I asked.

She explained that before they could fertilize the new grass, they had to rake up all the dead grass that lay unseen on the ground between the green blades. "If they don't," she said, "these new shoots won't last. The air and water and sunshine and fertilizer won't ever get down to their roots."

What a parallel, I thought, with the lives of many Christians. On the surface they look green and healthy, yet they are not coming into the identities God has for them. Areas of "dead grass" must be thatched before God's love can fully do its work.

The dead grass comes in many forms, but a major category can be termed simply "lies."

The Bible tells us that there is a real enemy of our souls, the spirit-being Satan, once the beloved archangel Lucifer, who through pride rebelled against God and who now spends his time trying to thwart His purposes. Satan's signature is to be found everywhere in human misery, but one of his main targets is the human mind, its thoughts and emotions. Jesus called him "the father of lies" (John 8:44), and he certainly lives up to his name, spreading lies about God and about ourselves that keep us from being all that God designed us to be.

THE CENTRAL LIE

John and Paula Sandford, in their book on inner healing, *The Transformation of the Inner Man*, identify a lie that infests every human life. As infants, they write, we learn that "good" behavior wins approval and demonstrations of love; "bad" behavior reaps the opposite, and we translate that to mean: "If I don't do right, I won't be loved. If I can't be what mommy and daddy want, I won't belong." This fear of rejection leads to what the Sandfords term "performance orientation," a mentality that forces us to strive to master the acceptable standards of whatever group we find ourselves in.[1]

The inevitable result of such constant adaptation is difficulty in finding our true identity. The greater tragedy is that this lie opens us to a more insidious lie: that *God's* love is like human love—conditional upon our performance. We are acceptable, we reason, only if we do the proper works. This is the impetus, of course, for all "religious" activity; man strives to win the favor or placate the wrath of whatever god he perceives.

But it contradicts everything in the Bible. Our God cries out to us repeatedly from His Word: "It is by *faith* that you are saved—faith in My Son Jesus and His perfect righteousness—*not* by your works!" We may nod in agreement, sing another chorus of "Amazing Grace" and then resume our religious activities as usual. When we remain in this kind of "relationship" with God, even subconsciously, we are open to accepting the assaults of the enemy on God and on ourselves.

FALSE IMAGES OF GOD

The whole Bible is a revelation of the true character of God, and Jesus often expressed His mission as the vindication of His Father from the maligning work of Satan. "I have made Your name known," He prays. "If you have seen Me you have seen the Father," He insists to His disciples. "I and My Father are one." But if we believe that God's love is conditional like our parents' many of us draw the parallel even further, making Him in their imperfect image and, therefore, cannot receive Jesus' words.

The adult child of an alcoholic reads in the Bible that God is no respecter of persons, that He is merciful and utterly faithful; but subconsciously she suspects that God, like her earthly father, is actually a breaker of promises, undependable, weak, and even treacherous. In her heart she decides, "I must do it all for myself. I must look out for myself," and she misses the security of Christ's Lordship in her life.

A gifted Christian songwriter finds herself pregnant just as her career is moving forward. She is filled with irrational anger at God. In prayer she discovers that, subconsciously, she thinks her career is over; God is like her macho Italian father, who joked about keeping women "in their place— barefoot and pregnant."

A businessman, who just cannot "feel" the love of God, realizes that his own over-achieving and often-absent father has set a pattern that interferes with his own image of God.

These distortions must be revealed by the Holy Spirit and removed, or they will infect our relationship with God and prevent our trusting in Him to re-create us.

FALSE IMAGES OF OURSELVES

More often than not we have false images of ourselves that block out any clear perception of our true identities. Here are some of the most prevalent.

"I'M O.K., YOU'RE O.K."

One false image of ourselves sown by the enemy is rather paradoxical because it seems to be positive. We have seen in the story of Jacob that in order to receive our true identities, we must recognize the unworthiness of the old ones. This calls for a true repentance and renunciation of our old ways, so that God can cleanse and restore us.

What Satan does is to make us think we aren't so bad, after all. In the modern world he has fostered such a selection of euphemisms (literally, "good speech") for ugly acts, that we consistently fail to call things what they are. He has masked our sin in sanitized vocabulary to the extent that we may feel no real shame, even when we confess.

In our "doublespeak" we eschew God's terms and substitute our own: "We misspoke ourselves," confesses the White House press secretary. "You lied," says the Word of God. "We terminate pregnancies," say the abortion clinics. "You murder," says the Word of God. "We have meaningful relationships," say the sexually active. "You fornicate and commit adultery," says the Word of God. And Isaiah cries, "Woe to those who call evil good and good evil" (Isaiah 5:20).

No wonder that even in confessing we feel no relief. We have not truly "spoken in agreement" with God, the literal meaning of the word *confess*. Only when we are willing to look at sin the way God does, call sin by name, bluntly, face head-on the reality of the things we do—only then can we be washed whiter than snow according to God's promises. Only when we speak the truth about past and present sin can we enter into our true identities. We must pray, too, for the Holy Spirit to give us the gift of conviction, lest our words, though correct, be empty.

PERHAPS I'M NOT A CHRISTIAN AFTER ALL

Another tactic of the enemy also relates to performance orientation. When we sin, Satan rushes in to challenge our positional identity in Christ: "Are you *sure* you're a Christian? Would a real Christian have done what you just did?" We reason: "If I am still doing such and such, then perhaps I'm not a real Christian after all. . . ." (Larry Tomczak observes in *Clap Your Hands* that Satan often whispers in the first person: "*I* must be the only person who thinks this way. . . . I'll bet *I'm* the only person who ever falls into this sin. . . .")

Haunted by the notion that we must earn our acceptance, we fall into his clutches, filled with doubt and anxiety.

But once we recognize the enemy's strategies, we can find our answer to his assaults in the Word, as Jesus did in the wilderness (see Luke 4, Matthew 4, Mark 1). *"If* you are the Son of God," hissed Satan. "It is written. . . ," answered Jesus, time and time again wielding the Sword of the Spirit against His accuser. When by the Holy Spirit we identify special areas of weakness, we can assemble an arsenal of Scriptures to combat the enemy and to remind ourselves of our true identity in Christ.

THOSE FAMILY MYTHS AND POISON NICKNAMES

Family myths are those pronouncements made upon children by lofty matriarchs (like maiden aunts)—or even by mothers and fathers—that, true or not, get etched somewhere in granite and can haunt us all of our lives. "Oh, yes," someone decrees, "William's the bright one in this family" (as his sisters and brothers, whose grades are equally good, gnash their teeth in indignation). Or, "Florence is as shy as her father—she'll never set the world on fire, that's for sure!" "May's temper is just like her grandmother's. She'll sure have trouble keeping a husband!" "Joe'll never amount to anything—he has his father's devil-may-care attitude."

We chafe with embarrassment or squirm with jealousy while such words burn deep into our subconscious, as damaging in their way as if they had been curses addressed to us from the deathbed of some wild-eyed Old Testament patriarch. Later, as we read the Lord's Word, "You are righteous and beloved and precious in My sight," we hear it through static: "You never apply yourself!" "You're the laziest person I ever saw!" "You're so stubborn, so bullheaded, so. . . ." You can fill in the blank.

Like myths, nicknames can linger throughout our entire lives, consciously forgotten, perhaps, but pumping poison just like a bee's stinger. "You are fashioned in My image, flawless," says the Lord, and in our memories we hear: "Fatty, Fatty, two by four. Can't get through the bathroom door!" Or, "Hey, Beanpole! How's the weather up there?" Or, "Hey, Ski-nose!"

A petite friend of mine never feels totally attractive because of an offhand remark by her boyfriend's mother nearly thirty years ago: "It's too bad she has such heavy legs!" Another beautiful friend still thinks of herself as "Bird-legs." (It didn't help matters, she says, that her last name was Partridge.) A handsome redheaded man sometimes see his boyish face in the mirror and hears the playground taunt: "Hey, Howdy Doody!"

Because "death and life are in the power of the tongue" (Proverbs 18:21), Satan can load seemingly harmless, even affectionate remarks with such powerful venom that even after an incident is long over, the words are still pumping poison into our systems. This is what sends many people into analysis, where they learn to spot the lie, but rarely find how to escape it. Knowing the dimensions of our cell doesn't set us free. In fact, someone has likened a bad self-image to a tar baby—the more we play with it, the more bound we are to it. Only the Holy Spirit working in His gentle power can pull the stinger on these lies and set us free to receive the new identity God has for us. When this is done, God has promised in Psalm 18:45 that "foreigners . . . [shall come] trembling out of their fastnesses." The lies, the distortions of our self-image, the distortions of God's identity, all those Satanic obstacles must, at the Word of God, forsake their strongholds in our minds and hearts.

MY TOO-GREAT EXPECTATIONS

We have spoken of those things that are hurtful and easily renounced, but not all of the things that keep us from our true identities are diabolical in origin. Some come from the world around us, from the people that we know and love, but their power is no less destructive. The ambitions of loving and well-meaning parents, the pull of friendship, the weight of family tradition, rigid cultural values and expectations, or seemingly noble duties can be just as strangling as a curse to our true selves.

In order to shape Abraham into the new man He wanted him to be, God had to call him out of his father's house and out of his own country into a place where God's values and plans reigned. Jacob met God and began to change only after he found himself alone, stripped of the security of old definitions and relationships. Peter had to leave his nets and, for a time, his family to fulfill his destiny, and Paul, as we have seen, lost all of these elements of identity for the sake of becoming God's person.

Why is this necessary? Because our "world," whatever and wherever it is, requires us to play roles, to acquire "personages," in Paul Tournier's phrase. We thus spend a lifetime assembling a wardrobe of masks. The expectations of others enslave us, subtly dictating how we think, talk, dress, where we live, what we buy, what professions we choose to follow, how we relate to each other. Gradually but surely we can lose any sense of who we are, what we want, what satisfies and truly fulfills *us*.

For some it is the expectations of a series of authority figures—parents, teachers, religious leaders—that shape the personage; for others, it may be a single dominant personality, a strong parent or teacher perhaps who, like the fictional Svengali, catches others in his or her own orbit. I grew up as an only child in close relationship with five very strong adults: my mother and father, my uncle, and my maternal grandparents. Their expectations were rarely if ever articulated; in fact, the only directives I remember were "just do the best you can," and "we just want you to be happy." These signals were, however, mixed with human and, therefore, conditional displays of approval. Wanting to please and fulfill their aspirations for me, I learned very early what kind of behavior would produce such approval. The trouble was, I believed each wanted something different.

My father, a writer and rather an iconoclast, valued articulate honesty above all else. He encouraged me to say what was on my mind. My mother, while valuing independent thinking, came down on the side of conventional behavior and the preservation of the "social graces." For my grandfather, a rancher-businessman, whose real love was his cattle and his land, I wanted to be brave and resourceful. For my uncle, a very bright and cultured person, I tried to be an intellectual. In the midst of all this, my grandmother, a lady straight out of *Gone with the Wind*, was trying her best to make me into a Southern belle ("Pretty is as pretty does!"). Trying to be all things to all people, I sometimes felt like a chameleon on plaid. When at last I was on my own, it took me many years and the Lord's healing wisdom to sort through the "oughts" and the "shoulds" for myself.

The need to separate, to become one's own person, is a healthy drive that psychologists assert is a necessary stage in human development. Ideally, in the time of separating a person weighs the lessons and values taught in childhood and makes a commitment to those he finds personally valuable and valid. Often it is also a time of rebellion against and rejection of those expectations we feel have been unfairly placed upon us by others.

The irony is that often, whether in adolescence or in mid-life (if our separation has not been accomplished earlier), this rebellion catapults us into a counterculture as rigidly structured as the one we are trying to leave. It has its own archetypal figures, its philosophy, its values, and its external expressions, like dress and jargon. We have all seen, and perhaps participated in, the great rebellion of the '60s when "flower children" rejected middle-class materialism, only to find themselves crammed into the equally restrictive patterns of the drug culture. (By the same token, some of the "hippies" are now, in fact, "yuppies," having traded personages again.) Without a savior to break the cycle, many ricochet from one set of conformities to the other, in a shifting but never-ending series of bondages.

The supreme irony is that we don't completely desire to leave our bondages, no matter how abhorrent they've become. In his famous soliloquy Hamlet observes that we "rather bear those ills we have than fly to those we know not of." The children of Israel, finally freed from a totally oppressive background, continued to yearn for the fleshpots of Egypt. The rich young ruler, drawn to the Lord Jesus, nevertheless walked away sadly when it became clear that he would have to forsake his family's wealth in order to gain the Kingdom. Lot, though daily grieved by the immorality of his city, Sodom, had to be torn away before its destruction by a delegation of angels, and his wife lost her life as she turned back in longing for the familiarity of home. Only the Lord can carve from us those "chains we cannot see," as Keith Green expressed it.

Jesus, issuing the radical call of the Gospel to leave all and find the Kingdom, met with a series of excuses:

> To another he said, "Follow me." But he said, "Lord, let me first go and bury my father." But he said to him, "Leave the dead to bury their own dead; but as for you, go and proclaim the kingdom of God." Another said, "I will follow you, Lord; but let me first say farewell to those at my home." Jesus said to him, "No one who puts his hand to the plow and looks back is fit for the kingdom of God."
>
> Luke 9:59–62

And another time He told a parable of a man who invited many to a great banquet:

> But they all alike began to make excuses. The first said to him, "I have bought a field, and I must go out and see it; I pray you, have me excused." And another said, "I have bought five yoke of oxen, and I go to examine them; I pray you, have me excused." And another said, "I have married a wife, and therefore I cannot come."
>
> Luke 14:18–20

Jesus' answer to these:

> If any one comes to me and does not hate his own father and mother and wife and children and brothers and sisters, yes, and even his own life, he cannot be my disciple.
>
> Luke 14:26

We are not to look back to the expectations of family or culture or education or even our own former ambitions. These words seem so harsh—one of the "hard sayings" of Jesus—that we try to explain it away. But it simply means that if we are to follow Jesus as Lord, we are not to follow any other, no matter how dear. He, of all people, calls for us to honor Father and Mother, to care for sisters, to be our brothers' keepers, to love and nurture our children. It is the excuse-making, procrastinating nature of the human heart that Jesus confronts.

Jesus knows, because He is the Designer, that the human spirit is able to serve only one master—Himself. Human beings cannot (not *should* not, but *cannot*) serve two masters (Matthew 6:24). Divided loyalties paralyze the growth of the spirit; and our loyalty to other human beings can be our place of greatest vulnerability to temptation. The stories of Adam and Eve, Abraham and Sarah, bear this out. Jesus Himself tasted the terrific power of the enemy through Peter's words when His beloved disciple tried to dissuade Him from obeying His Father and going to the cross (Matthew 16:23).

CONFORMITY IN THE KINGDOM

Kenneth S. Wuest in his expanded translation of the New Testament gives a clear, strong rendering from the literal Greek of the familiar passage, Romans 12:2:

> Stop assuming an outward expression that does not come from within you and is not representative of what you are in your inner being but is patterned after this age; but change your outward expression to one that comes from within and is representative of your inner being, by the renewing of your mind.[2]

As we read these words, believers most likely think of them as applying to our need to avoid the ungodly practices of the outside world. But what about pressures to conform *within the Kingdom*? How much of our Christian identity comes not from within but from the pressures without to look and talk and act like everyone else in our particular heritage or denomination. In some communities where ethnic origin and religion are tightly interwoven the influence is obvious, the pressure overt. In some like the Nazarene Church, for example, standards of dress and behavior are even written out. In others it is unspoken but operative. Those who breach taboos in their appearance or style of worship, or some other way, quickly get the message.

One area of conformity that exists even in the most enlightened churches, especially in these days of renewed interest in the proper roles of men and women, is sexual stereotypes. We *say*: "There is neither Jew nor Greek, there is neither slave nor free, there is neither male nor female; for you are all one in Christ Jesus" (Galatians 3:28), but we belie these Scriptures in subtle and not-so-subtle practices.

THE SUBMISSIVE WIFE

Perhaps the most oppressive teaching is that which distorts the godly ideal of husband-wife relationships. It seems to be a phenomenon within the Body of Christ that women are more receptive to spiritual things. Consequently, they delve more into Scripture or enter into prayer with more freedom than their husbands. Unfortunately, some women, being puffed up with knowledge (without wisdom) lord it over their husbands, making them feel like neophytes. Whatever the reason, the Body of Christ seems to have its share of super-spiritual women and browbeaten husbands who have abnegated their rightful place and responsibility within the home. To address this problem, many current teachings have focused on the Scriptures that tell wives and husbands how to relate to one another as God intends, giving general guidelines for mutual respect and love and protection and upbuilding. When properly understood and taught, these

verses are edifying and liberating to both men and women.
But when taught in a carnal spirit, influenced by old antag-
onisms, they can be destructive.

For example, Ephesians 5:21–33 is a beautiful picture of how
husbands and wives should relate to each other, starting with
an admonition to be subject to one another out of reverence for
Christ (honoring and trusting each other on the basis of His
worthiness), and ending with the charge to husbands to love
their wives as themselves and to wives to respect their husbands. Throughout the passage wives are called to "subject"
or "submit" themselves to their husbands. These are the
words used for a formation of Roman soldiers, whose mutual
submission in terms of their relative positions and in place-
ment of their shields meant safety from attack. When properly
taught, the passage deals with adaptation by the wives and
self-sacrificial love by the husbands—a godly management
system for the enrichment and joy of both partners.

In unbalanced teaching, however, the emphasis is thrown
squarely on two words: "Wives, submit" and the subsequent
interpretation can be anything from "adjust to your husband's ideas" to "submit yourself to any abuse, without
complaint." When these and other Scriptures are wrenched
from their textual and historical context, tainted with human
prejudice, and taught by the letter and not the spirit of the
Word, they become deadly. No longer descriptive of God's
best for both sexes, they are proscriptive and demeaning.

Worse still, the Submissive Wife stereotype is extended by
some to apply to all women, not just wives, perpetuating a
kind of chauvinism that denigrates all female believers and
dishonors the Lord. Ignoring the examples of God's powerful
use of such biblical leaders as Miriam, Deborah, and Priscilla,
ignoring Jesus' obvious respect for and friendship with
women like Mary and Martha, Joanna, and others of His
entourage, such teachings use God's Word to bludgeon
women into silence and inactivity (except in a limited sphere
of service).

The message comes across: A woman is to sit down, shut up, acquiesce to whatever a man tells her (not just her husband) and think of herself as a second-class citizen, even in the sight of God. She shouldn't teach or exercise gifts or leadership, lest she usurp a man's authority and dishonor God's Word. When this message hits a person who already struggles with a poor self-image or with confusion about her place in the Kingdom, it simply thrusts her, wounded and resentful, into a deeper level of unwholeness, into a bondage reinforced by what she thinks *God* thinks of her.

THE HIGH PRIEST

The High Priest stereotype (counterpart to the Submissive Wife) dictates that men operate autonomously, making unilateral decisions as Heads of the Households who rarely call upon the discernment of those who should be their most loving and trusted allies. Ironically, this kind of teaching, instead of enhancing a man's position, ultimately brings undue pressure on men in general and especially on husbands who are expected to be "spiritual honchos" without the benefit of their wives' help. As the wives are taught to turn off their own opinions, the men lose the benefit of their counsel; at the same time the women put so much pressure on the men that they break down trying to assume responsibilities they were never intended to carry alone.

I made this mistake with Michael early in our life together as Christians. At that point I did know more Scripture, but he was supposed to be the head of our household, and I was so afraid of overwhelming him with my opinions that I clammed up altogether. Watching him make decisions that I thought were mistakes, I pled to the Lord, "*You* tell him!" but inside I felt dishonest and frustrated. Finally, some crisis prompted us to a frank discussion and prayer time, and we rediscovered something we had forgotten—that we were *partners*, not adversaries, and that God had put us together to complete each other.

THE GOOD CHRISTIAN MOTHER

Another stereotype that wreaks havoc with us as we try to discover our true identities but wrestle with conformity within the Kingdom is that of the Good Christian Mother. My guess is that this role is patterned after Susanna Wesley, an eighteenth-century Englishwoman blessed by God with supernatural organizational skills (and nineteen children). We read that she spent special time with each child, *every day*, teaching not only skills for use in the world, but the ways of godliness. Among the "fruits of her labor" were her sons John and Charles who, respectively, preached sermons and wrote hymns that have glorified God for two centuries. Her example is truly inspiring to all believers.

But distorted, it takes on a life of its own. The archetype of the Good Christian Mother spends her total waking hours quoting or singing Scripture to her little one in a nursery papered with Bible figures (no Mother Goose for her). As the child grows (breast-fed and then weaned on homegrown, home-ground baby food) she is unfailingly consistent in exercising her authority (without usurping her husband's role). She never yells or loses her temper over the spilled apple juice or the soiled clothes. When she is not home-schooling, she bakes (with her child at her side), sews (and smocks) his clothes or directs art projects that simultaneously teach him to read and count. Her personal preferences are happily shelved for decades and she finds total fulfillment in the kitchen or the nursery. If she should happen to get away for an hour or two she suffers appropriate guilt.

SUPERWOMAN

The double whammy is that the Good Christian Mother is only one face of an even more overwhelming stereotype: Superwoman or the Proverbs Lady (described in Proverbs 31:10–31). Again, a wonderful, *general* pattern for *all* believers has been turned into a tyrannical set of criteria for women of the Kingdom. Already assaulted at every checkout counter with pressure from women's magazines, many Christian women burn out trying to fulfill all the biblical categories of activity and virtue without the anointing of God upon their efforts.

I had just finished a teaching about the "Proverbs Lady" to a group of young women in our church, trying to lift the description to a more spiritual level of application (for example, verse 18: "Her lamp does not go out at night" means that the Word is always with her as a light to her path, not that she never sleeps!). A conscientious new believer (an intern at a major teaching hospital in Washington and a new wife) came up to me in great distress. She had been embracing the Word with total enthusiasm and resolve but without the discernment of the Holy Spirit, and could no longer face what she thought the Lord was requiring from her. She wept tears of relief to discover that what our hearts cherish and desire to do, God counts as done, and that He who alone knows our capacities should set the pace for our lives, not a Christian cultural stereotype.

THE CHRISTIAN SUCCESS

In tracing pressures Christians feel to conform (thus making it difficult to find our own identity), the male counterpart to Superwoman is the Overachiever for Christ. This stereotype, shot through with the standards of the "prosperity gospel" (God wants His people in Cadillacs) seems based on an attempt to show those in the world that we Christians can outdo them at their own game. Excellence for Christ, top production in the marketplace, credible witness in the halls of power—these are indisputably admirable goals. But when these philosophies and standards are not personally anointed to a man's heart by the Holy Spirit, they can entice him into ways far from the Lord's methods. For some, this stereotype is far more dangerous, for it fans the flames of "worka-

holism" that may lie within, running the real risk of breaking
up marriages and wrecking lives.

These are but a few representative stereotypes that can
stifle individuality, but I believe they are typical. Built on
"good" guidelines, they may be worthy models. The trouble
is that they can be animated by a life of their own. They can
become implacable idols, putting unbearable pressure on
many believers, causing them to give up in despair and
rebellion or to toil away under constant condemnation,
cloning themselves to some impossible ideal and secretly
resenting God as a "hard taskmaster." We *must*, before
receiving teachings or even before reading so-called Christian
"self-help" books, pray for the guidance of the Holy Spirit,
lest we fall into imitating identities that are not our own.

THE ULTIMATE OBSTACLE: THE CHRISTIANS I CREATE

Before I learned that identity was to be God's gift, and not
my creation, I spent a lot of time trying to fashion a
"Christian identity." At various stages, it resembled different
things. At first I strove to be a Christian woman in the mold
of my mother and grandmother. This meant serving on any
church committee that beckoned, praying a certain number
of hours a day, making the inescapable cheese casseroles,
volunteering for civic works, and generally channeling my
limited energies into real ineffectiveness. When the Lord
finally reined me in from those activities, provided time for
me to learn the Bible, and showed me the work He had for
me to do, I thought I had been set free from this tendency to
design myself.

Unfortunately, when the Lord blessed us with our first
child, Meg, I then bought into the Good Christian Mother
stereotype. Initially I had feelings of moderate success,
although my best-laid plans to "be creative" oft got pre-
empted by the spilled apple juice. As Meg grew older,
however, and I encountered her emerging will in all its fallen

human strength, I went into a kind of decline, frustrated by my inability to do "it" the way I thought God was wanting "it" done. After months of suffering guilt and feelings of inadequacy, I finally asked the Lord to help me understand what I was doing wrong. In my prayer time, as I walked a nearby golf course, He spoke to my heart: "You've gathered together a real killer-composite of Christian ideals piled on top of women's magazine standards. No wonder you have no joy! Would you like *My* definition of a 'good mother'? I want you to be honest, not perfect, and I want you to be openly dependent on Me, so that Meg will learn her real source of wisdom." And then He said the most liberating thing of all, which I still treasure: "I gave this child to you because you are who you are. Your strengths will be her example and her protection; your weaknesses will be the catalysts to develop *her* own strengths. The perfect mother for her is *you*, because I designed you for one another."

I'd like to be able to say that I learned my lesson from that gracious encounter. In the years since, however, I have many times assembled new graven images, carved from my own pride, new composites of Mother Teresa, Joan of Arc, Catherine Marshall, and various friends whom I admire. But the Lord doesn't let me live under their dominion for too long, for He is a jealous God, and will tolerate no idols. When I begin to think that my tasks are too much, that my burden is *not* light and that His grace is *not* sufficient, I am learning to check to see if the expectations are His or mine. He's always glad to show me!

Oswald Chambers warns that one of the most dangerous things we can do as believers is to be "set on our own way for God."[3] So much has been done in the Lord's name that has not been at His bidding! Even those who would encourage us to "imitate Jesus" must remember that *our* "Jesuses" can be very far off the mark. The secret to our identity, our perfect fulfillment of the place God has designed specifically for us, is to be like Jesus in this one thing: To do only those things that He tells us, just as He did and said only those things that

He heard and saw His Father doing (John 8:28). All else is fueled by "strange fire" and will remain outside the circle of His blessing. All that we do, writes Chambers, should "be founded on a perfect oneness with Him, not a self-willed determination to be godly."

7

GROWING INTO YOUR NAME

Even though we are new creatures, the old nature still wants to dictate terms. Our natural desire for autonomy dies hard, so a great part of growing into our new identities, letting our new names settle into our hearts, is yielding to the Lord as Creator and Re-Creator, whether we understand His ways or not. To those who question God's designs Isaiah relays His indignant response:

> *You turn things upside down! Shall the potter be regarded as the clay; that the thing made should say of its maker, "He did not make me"; or the thing formed say of him who formed it, "He has no understanding"?*
> Isaiah 29:16

To our spiritual selves such arrogance is almost comical, and we wouldn't suspect ourselves of harboring similar protests. Nevertheless, deep in our hearts we may have to work at accepting God's design for us and our place in His Kingdom.

THE PART PHYSICAL APPEARANCE PLAYS

Though we may not recognize them as such, our physical selves are equipment for ministry. God has created each of us in a unique way, outside as well as inside, to do and be certain things. The trouble is, the influence of the world's frenetic quest for youth and beauty is impossible to escape, and what the world defines as desirable is confined to a very narrow spectrum. (By worldly standards, many of the world's most beautiful women consider themselves ugly.) So, thousands *spend* thousands on such drastic measures as plastic surgery and hair transplants while millions spend billions on cosmetics, strenuous dieting programs, body-building courses. Few of us seem pleased with what we were issued.

In fact, I have heard it said that much alienation from God in young people stems from their dissatisfaction with their physical appearance during the awkward period of adolescence. They reason: "If God made me, and I'm such a disaster, how 'good' a God can He be?"

Like the destructive words that fester, half-forgotten, in our subconscious, feelings of physical inadequacy and distrust of our Creator can remain undetected in our hearts for years. For some it is difficult to admit that such concerns affect a matter so spiritual as our relationship to God. Indeed, some "attributes" like being overweight or washed-out-looking may be things we can change; we are, after all, stewards of the temples of our bodies as well as of our time and money.

But it may be that the Lord can help us to "accept those things we cannot change" by showing us how such attributes equip us for service. For example, it can be seen that attributes of God's people in the Bible are often crucial to the part they play in the unfolding of His will. Moses was a stutterer ("slow of speech," is how he puts it, Exodus 4:10–11), and was, therefore, highly reluctant to be God's spokesman before Pharaoh and his court. God reminded him that since He had made Moses' mouth in the first place, He could also make it work. But in a gracious concession to Moses' continuing fears, God gave Moses his own brother Aaron as partner. This experience in shared leadership prepared Aaron for his role as the future first High Priest of Israel.

A strange story in Judges 3:12–30 tells of Ehud, a man from the tribe of Benjamin, whom God used to deliver Israel from the oppression of Eglon, king of Moab. Because Ehud was left-handed, the king's men missed the sword he carried; with it, he killed the king and escaped to safety.

Ironically, Esther may have rued her physical beauty, for because of it she was taken into the harem of a pagan king; yet it was this same beauty that gave her favor with him, and enabled her to be the agent of her people's salvation.

Paul, as we have seen, learned to celebrate his small physical stature because he saw that God's glory might well be better demonstrated in a man who was not naturally imposing. As God had told Samuel when He sent him to anoint another small man, David, for kingship: "For the Lord sees not as man sees; man looks on the outward appearance, but the Lord looks on the heart" (1 Samuel 16:7).

In my hometown, to be beautiful was to be cheerleader-petite. Being very tall, I naturally struggled most of my life with the "problem" of my height. Wanting more to observe than to *be* observed, I suffered agonies of self-consciousness, especially during my teenage years. When I came into the Kingdom, I discovered that height caused some to look to me for leadership and forced me to develop skills that might have remained dormant had God given me my wish to be "average."

A dear friend of mine had the opposite "problem." Being a very tiny person (in a family of thirteen children!) she was often resentful that no one ever seemed to pay attention to her. The desire to be noticed as "one of a kind" has developed in her traits of leadership as well as compassion for others who seem "lost in the crowd." Another friend, a man with a physical handicap, was never able to play the same sports as other boys. It could have made him bitter and isolated. Instead, it caused him to develop an extraordinary wit and the capacity to empathize with others who are different. They, too, have learned from the Lord that the things they once saw only as liabilities have been the very things that give them special credibility and favor with the people to whom God has ordained them to minister.

We may not have obvious features that we consider problems, but most of us wish we were different in some way: "I wish I were taller . . . or blonde like my sister," or "Why did I inherit Dad's big nose? or Mother's weak chin?" Those who *are* "average" may lament that there is nothing outstanding about their physical appearance. We all can take immense comfort in remembering that the Son of God Himself "had no form or comeliness that we should look at him, and no beauty that we should desire him . . ." (Isaiah 53:2). It was the beauty of holiness within Him that acted like an irresistible magnet, pulling the crowds to Him, causing them to declare Him "altogether lovely" (Song of Solomon 5:16).

Jesus asked, rhetorically, "Which of you by taking thought can add one cubit to his stature?" (Matthew 6:27, KJV). We may never ever meet the world's standards of beauty, but we *can* take on the same loveliness of the Master we serve, till our appearance takes its proper place on the list of priorities. Or we may find that, as usual, the Master Designer knew exactly what He was doing when He framed our particular packaging. God knows that perfection is hard to warm up to; the imperfections of His people should make us approachable to those who spy the Lord inside. The receding hairline, the slightly uneven teeth, even the dreaded cellulite, may give someone the courage to ask us about the God we serve, who loves us even though we're just "ordinary" people.

ACCEPTING OUR MISSION FIELDS

The once-popular television show *Mission: Impossible* regularly opened with these words issuing from a classified tape recording: "Your mission, Jim—should you decide to accept it . . ." Even though the assignments were always, as the title said, "impossible," to my knowledge "Jim" never refused. But many times *we* balk at the mission God has given us. The classic fear of fledgling Christians—that God will immediately send us to darkest Africa—soon fades as we realize that instead, God may be keeping us in darkest Fairfax, Virginia, or Orlando, Florida, or wherever we happen to be. The place and the people we are called to serve, or the way in which we are called to serve them, may not at first suit our idea of what ought to be happening. We may feel like Jacob, working to earn Rachel and getting Leah instead.

Paul, for example, as we have seen, was sent to the Gentiles, when every bit of logic would dictate his going to his own Hebrew people. All his scholarship, his stunning knowledge of the Old Testament, and his trained powers of persuasion seemed to aim him at those People of the Promise who could fully appreciate his arguments and teaching. Of course, God knew that the power that brought people into the Kingdom had nothing to do with human eloquence or knowledge. Only when Paul was relying totally on and operating in the power of the Holy Spirit could people's understanding be opened to the Gospel. Paul came to know that preaching that was half-Spirit and half-intellect would never win the souls so precious to Christ, and he obediently answered God's call to the nations of Gentiles.

When Jonah found himself directed to preach to the Ninevites, who were ancient and despised enemies of his people, he caught the first boat heading in the opposite direction. But God moved the sea itself and one of its largest citizens to deliver Jonah to his assignment. To his surprise the Ninevites repented, and even then God had to give a further lesson in compassion, challenging the petulant prophet: "And should not I pity Nineveh, that great city, in which there are more than a hundred and twenty thousand persons who do not know their right hand from their left?" (Jonah 4:11).

Jill Briscoe, British evangelist now ministering with her husband in America, was a student at Oxford in the early '60s when she met Jesus Christ as Lord, and her heart yearned for the conversion of other young people. But instead of a youth ministry, her first "assignment" was a church group of little old ladies. She cried out to the Lord that there must be some mistake. But God knew what He was doing. As they began to love and trust Jill these little old ladies began sending their teenaged grandchildren to her. Before long she had a team of kids who would accompany her on missions into nightclubs of cities like Liverpool. While kids listened to the emerging rock-'n'-roll groups like the Beatles, Jill and her team sat at their tables and told them the good news of Jesus Christ and His love for them. God, knowing the demographics of that particular church, had first laid a foundation for her ministry.[1]

AVOIDING THE COMPARISON TRAP

As we looked at the life of Peter we saw that the Lord had prepared individual paths for each of His disciples; Peter was admonished to focus his attention on following the Lord, not to be concerned about John's future (John 21:21–22). As their lives began to unfold Peter must have thought of Jesus' answer many times, as he saw the Lord employing his fellow disciples in so many different ways.

Even though their preparation had been the same, their Lord had been the same, and their fate had been fairly much the same in their days as disciples, when they were sent out as apostles, their unique contributions became clear. As one suffered prison, the other led huge revivals; as one was put to death, the other's ministry prospered. Probably by that time they all understood the truth that God's ways are sovereign and sometimes mysterious. They each "had so much on their plates," as we used to say in Texas, that they didn't have too much time to quarrel over what He was assigning to whom, as they had in the early days.

Unfortunately, many of us in the modern-day Body of Christ have not yet learned that lesson. And we spend much of our time consciously or unconsciously looking at our neighbor, seeing only from the outside and comparing ourselves and our walks with theirs.

Paul illustrates the problems this creates in his famous analogy of the Body of Christ to the human body:

> *God arranged the organs in the body, each one of them, as he chose. If all were a single organ, where would the body be? . . . The eye cannot say to the hand, "I have no need of you," nor again the head to the feet, "I have no need of you."*   1 Corinthians 12:18–21

SUPERIOR AND INFERIOR

When we compare ourselves we often fall into one of two traps: superiority or inferiority. Jesus told the story of the Pharisee and the publican (Luke 18:9–14) to illustrate the insidious danger of the pride of *superiority*. Looking at the tax collector entering the Temple at the same time as he was, the Pharisee stood before God and "prayed": "God, I thank thee that I am not like other men, extortioners, unjust, adulterers, or even like this tax collector. I fast twice a week, I give tithes of all that I get." The publican, despised as a traitor by his people for being in the employ of Rome, dared not even lift his eyes to heaven, much less look around at his fellow-worshipers: "God, be merciful to me a sinner!" was all he could manage. Yet Jesus tells us that it was he who was counted right in God's sight, for he had held himself to the real standard of comparison: the holiness of God Himself.

The law is: Everyone who exalts himself will be humbled, but he who humbles himself will be exalted.

The arrogant "eye" in Paul's illustration fails to appreciate the "hand" and falls into the sin of pride, missing the truth that the function of the whole depends on each member doing his or her part. "If one member suffers, all suffer together; if one member is honored, all rejoice together" (1 Corinthians 12:26). This is not a directive; it is a fact. We are organically linked in the spiritual realm, and if we regard anyone as less than crucial to our welfare we are making a very foolish mistake.

Conversely, many in the Body of Christ make the opposite mistake and think of ourselves as inferior. Observing from the outside (with limited vision) we watch the ministry and character of another and, comparing ourselves, we come up short. We do not see the trials in their lives, the frustrations, the battles that God says are going on in each life. All we see is the glamorous ministry, the appearance of "having it all together." "I am not an eye," we pout; "there is no need for me." And in our self-pity, we build a highway for the enemy to drive a whole convoy of ugly spiritual tanks between us, our sisters and brothers, and our God. We resent God: Why didn't He make me thus and so? Why didn't He give me the same opportunities as so-and-so? If I only had so-and-so's money or free time or . . . And then we let resentment, jealousy, anger crowd out all natural affection.

In Numbers 12, jealousy over ministry came near to being the downfall of a powerful man and woman. It is recorded that Moses' sister, Miriam, and his brother, Aaron, began to murmur against their brother, asking: "Has the Lord indeed spoken only through Moses? Has he not spoken through us also?" The Lord dealt harshly, especially with Miriam, for yielding to these devilish feelings, and it was only after Moses' intercession that harmony was restored within their family.

In the story of the very first brothers it was jealousy and envy of Abel's favor in God's sight that caused Cain to hate and finally to murder his brother. God was no respecter of persons—He said outright to Cain that if he did right he would have favor, too—but Cain's eyes were on his brother and the enemy was able to poison his soul against him. We may not commit murder, even in our hearts, but if our eyes are fixed enviously on other people we will denigrate them to others, we will withhold our prayers for them, we will certainly be alienated from them, and we will fail to recognize that *their* strengths can bless *us*.

A beautiful woman I know, whose life in the Lord as a mother, artist, lover of poetry, and intercessor is a role model for many, was recently honored on her seventy-fifth birthday by her thirteen children and forty-nine of her fifty grandchildren, most of whom are believers. An idyllic picture, but she confided that times had not always been easy. Betty had married a man she knew would soon become an invalid, and they began their large family early in their marriage. She had some help with the household chores, but was nevertheless many times physically worn down and stretched to her emotional limits by all her little ones.

When her mother-in-law would arrive to distract the children with games and talk and excursions, my friend confessed that her gratitude was tainted by envy. "She's so good with the children," she would say to herself, "and I'm so frustrated and angry and bad with them. They'd be much better off without me!" She was near despair when the Lord finally got her to see that her mother-in-law's talent with the kids was meant as a blessing for all of them. How many blessings do we miss because we feel competitive toward sisters and brothers rather than receiving their ministry as a gracious gift from the Lord?

Another trouble with having our eyes on each other rather than on the Lord is that, especially if we're new Christians, we may fall into slavish imitation of the lifestyle, the ministry, even the personality of the Christians around us. Their devotional lives, their taste, their outlook often seems so

"Christlike" that we work to replicate *them* rather than listening for our own orders.

I have fallen into this trap so many times that I know its dimensions intimately. My first Scripture teacher was so radically committed to the Lord that I thought I had to do all that she did—and her ministry was prodigious. While I struggled just to read through the Bible, I often felt guilty that I couldn't be as productive as she—teaching, counseling, typing sermons, distributing, buying and sending books and tapes to countless believers. Another friend, a teacher with a dynamic personality, had a photographic memory for all the Old Testament kings and wars and geography. I could barely keep straight when the Northern and the Southern kingdoms divided, much less when and where everyone went into exile. Or I'd look at one of our ministers, a vibrant and charming young man whose voice and manner were, I thought, perfect instruments to convey the deep things of God. I would listen to my puny Texas-accented voice on tape and wince. "What good am I?" I would sigh. "I don't have Barbara's energy or Theresa's memory or Jeff's charismatic personality." Finally, the Lord spoke: "If I'd wanted clones of your friends, don't you think I could've made them? *Follow thou Me!*"

In this regard we are sometimes confused by a certain injunction of Paul's: "I urge you, then, be imitators of me," Paul wrote to the Corinthians (1 Corinthians 4:16), and he often urged his protegé, Timothy, to look to him as an example, but he meant in terms of virtue, not in personality. We know that because Paul also constantly urged Timothy to pursue and grow in the gifts, the walk, and the ministry he had been given by God. Paul knew that we do need role models when we first begin to live the Christian life— "discipling" is a legitimate endeavor—but he was always scrupulous to point Timothy toward his Lord. When someone eclipses the Lord Himself as the one we look to for direction and approval, we sorely miss the mark. In fact, it seems that there comes a time in every discipling relationship

when the Lord's direction will call for our loyalties to be
tested, and woe to the teacher or leader who has so imposed
his or her own style on the disciple that the student can't
follow gladly and confidently after his Lord. Our watchword
should be the words of John the Baptist when he was told
that some of his followers were "deserting" him to follow
after Jesus. Wisely, he answered, "He must increase, but I
must decrease" (John 3:30). God help us to remember that as
we try to teach and counsel others!

STEWARDING OUR GIFTS

In Matthew 25:14–30 Jesus told the story of a man who was
going away and who entrusted to his servants his property,
giving to one one talent, another two, and another five, each
according to his ability. Two of the servants invested and
traded and doubled their property. But the one who had
received only one talent did nothing but hide it, explaining
later to his master that because he "knew" the master was a
hard man, he had been afraid to risk losing it. The master
exposes sloth as the man's real motivation: "If you 'knew' I
was such a hard man, all the more reason to increase what I
entrusted to you!"

Many lessons are contained in this parable, but the basic
truth is that whatever gift, ministry, and identity we have,
they are actually the property of someone else, the living
God. Being creatures and not our own creators, we are only
the stewards of our lives; we are accountable to the One who
has entrusted them to us. Peter recognized this truth, writing:
"As each has received a gift, employ it for one another as
good stewards of God's varied grace . . ." (1 Peter 4:10).

So what are God's directions to us on the "spending" of
ourselves (our gifts, our time, our thoughts and emotions)?
Generally speaking, His charge to us is to spend ourselves
freely. Everywhere in Scripture the Creator Himself and His
works are spoken of in terms of their abundance: "I came that
they may have life, and have it abundantly" (John 10:10); He

is "able to do far more abundantly than all that we ask or think" (Ephesians 3:20). His self-portrait in the story of the Prodigal Son is of a profligate father, pouring out upon the bowed head of his penitent son the riches of his merciful love, showering welcome gifts. The psalmists compare His blessings with rainfall, and describe Him as almost wanton in His creativity.

In the parable of the talents the master commends those who spent and multiplied their money. "Freely ye received, freely give," Jesus instructed His disciples (Matthew 10:8), and the law of the Kingdom of God is "give, and it will be given to you. . . . For the measure you give will be the measure you get back" (Luke 6:38).

In appealing for the support of the church in Jerusalem, Paul writes:

The point is this: he who sows sparingly will also reap sparingly, and he who sows bountifully will also reap bountifully. Each one must do as he has made up his mind, not reluctantly or under compulsion, for God loves a cheerful giver. And God is able to provide you with every blessing in abundance, so that you may always have enough of everything and may provide in abundance for every good work.

2 Corinthians 9:6–8

We are thus assured that if we will cheerfully be spent for the blessing of God's people, He will give back the love and the energy it has cost us, just as He "opens the windows of heaven" to those who tithe their material resources (Malachi 3:10).

One caveat is in order. Many gifted people, zealously wanting to obey this general direction of the Lord, find themselves in the dangerous situation of not knowing how to say no to requests for ministry. The cry "But you're the only one who can chair this committee or design this newsletter or teach this class" carries great power. Burn-out is not something that only occurs in the so-called secular world. Many a pastor or hostess or mother or administrator or preacher has spread him or herself so thin as to be of no use to anyone. How then do we learn to say no? Is it ever legitimate?

Looking in the Bible, we find that Jesus Himself said no on occasion. Legion were the requests upon Him for what only He could deliver. The call of "duty" upon a heart as noble as His, the tug of yearning in His compassionate spirit must have been agonizing temptations to go to everyone who called out. The key to selective intercession is obedience. Jesus' allegiance was to one voice only—that of His Father. He knew that the Father alone had the wisdom to orchestrate help to the needs around Him. So when word came that His beloved cousin and friend, John, was imprisoned by Herod, He did not go, though it must have torn at His heart to stay where He was (Matthew 11:1–6). When Lazarus, an equally close friend, lay ill and dying, His Father did not bid Him go, and so Jesus tarried, understanding that the best plan of God called for His refusal to intervene (John 11:1–44).

We, too, if we would be the stewards God wants us to be, must also be willing to look to Him for a yes or a no, as a handmaiden keeps her eyes on her mistress for direction. So many times we want to rush in and fill the need we see, thinking, "But, of course, God wants this done. . . ." The mature steward, however, knows that his Master's timing, the "fullness of time," is often a more key factor than the action itself.

In the prophet Ezekiel God found a servant sensitive and yielded enough that He could call upon him to lie still— literally. In Ezekiel 4:4 God calls him to be a living parable to the house of Israel, to lie upon his left side for 390 days as a symbol of the years of punishment Israel faces, and then turn over and lie upon his right side for 40 days as a symbol of the years of punishment in store for Judah. What a challenge to those of us who find it difficult to "do nothing"!

But surely we have seen or tasted "burn-out" enough to realize that our enemy loves to dissipate our energies on tasks that are not God-ordained. What better way to keep us from real stewardship than to send calls upon our time that will be unfruitful. Paul Yonggi Cho, pastor of the largest church in the world, in Seoul, Korea, warns also of people he calls "energy monsters." These are people with real needs who unwittingly aid the work of the enemy by wearing out those servants who don't yet know how to check out requests with the real Master.

Our distractions will not be racetracks and things of the world; they may well be "good works," like taking over Vacation Bible School "just one more year. . . ." We need to learn that before we agree to help, we must consult with the Lord, lest we become led by wrong motives (duty, guilt, experience, ego, messianic tendencies) into empty work, and fail to do the works God has prepared for us and us alone. Our hearts and hands are to be perpetually open, eager to give, but our ears must be open, too, to the Master's yes or no directions.

HELPING OTHERS GROW INTO THEIR NEW NAMES

In Numbers 11:26–30, a young man rushes to report to Moses that two of the elders of Israel are prophesying in the camp. Joshua, Moses' "assistant," urges him to forbid them. But Moses answers, "Are you jealous for my sake? Would that all the Lord's people were prophets, that the Lord would put his spirit upon them!" (Numbers 11:29). Moses was so secure in his own relationship with God and in his ministry that it was no threat to him or his identity if others came into their own. He was delighted to see and help others move into their places. How can we do the same?

Taking Jesus as our model, we can begin to *try to see others in their new identities:* as Jesus addressed the still old-self Simon as Peter, so we can see others for what they *will* be and begin to treat them as if they already were those things. How? By being faithful to give them encouragement for those emerging attributes we recognize as being the Lord's work in them. By exhorting those who are timid about stepping out into new ministry. By being willing to share our experience. By praying for them.

Paul wrote about the fact that once he regarded Jesus of Nazareth as simply another human person. But no longer, he declared to the Corinthians: "From now on, therefore, we regard no one from a human point of view" (2 Corinthians 5:16). What does it mean "to regard others from a human point of view"? For one thing it means to imprison them in their pre-Christian identities, relating to them as if they were still living under the dominion of darkness, ruled by old motivations. My husband and I have to be very careful with statements that begin "You always" and "You never" for these express what we used to be, not what we are becoming.

Once Michael had made an especially thorny response to something in a church committee meeting. As we drove home, I was tempted to nag him to practice a little diplomacy. *Why does he always . . .* I began in my head, but the Lord stopped me, conveying to my heart that Michael's bluntness was going to be transformed into an honesty by which he would render unique service in the Kingdom. *He's a son of thunder now,* the Lord said to my heart, *but I plan to make him a son of encouragement.* I understood then that I could keep him imprisoned in his old ways by my criticism or set him free by sharing God's vision of him. We must allow each other the freedom to change—daily—and to respond to the sanctifying work of the Holy Spirit, refusing to condemn them to a life of unchanging carnality.

David was commended by God for his attitude toward Saul. Even after the King had become a madman, trying at every turn to murder David, the younger man refused to slay his pursuer: "Who can put forth his hand against the Lord's anointed, and be guiltless?" (1 Samuel 26:9). The Lord had anointed Saul, and David respected him for what he had the potential to be. When we are born again, we have to remember that each of us is new. And we must make a conscious effort not to call each other by our old "names."

Viewing people as God views them means refusing to categorize them—by sex, denomination, ethnic background, or whatever else the world uses to classify and, thereby, dehumanize people. Jamie Buckingham in his book *Risky Living: Keys to Inner Healing* tells of a time he spent at a Methodist church camp. In his zeal for the Lord he was frustrated with what he thought was their entrenched denominationalism. Deep in his heart he judged them as being caught up in religiosity rather than in personal relationships with his beloved Jesus Christ. One morning very early he went out to pray at a giant cross that had been built near the lake.

I don't know how long I stood there, arms outstretched, hands pressed against those rough, splintering beams. Gradually, though, I began to tire. My shoulders ached and my arms were weary. But I would not take them down. I wanted to stay on forever where my Lord had hung.

I felt my arms falling and reached for the top of the crossbeams to hold on. Each second seemed meaningful. But as I gripped the tops of the cross bars, I noticed something strange. The texture of the wood was different. On the sides it was rough, rugged. On top it was smooth.

Painfully, I realized what it meant. I was not the first to put myself against that cross. Countless others—those Methodists whom I had criticized as "un-godly" and "un-spiritual"—had been there before me. By the hundreds. Perhaps thousands. It was their tired hands which had worn the wood smooth.

I returned to camp, chastened. . . .[2]

The Lord has often showed me that I, too, classify and condemn with alarming ease. In personal relationships and in times of counseling and praying with people the Lord has had to call me to repent over and over for the prejudices I have in my heart toward a person's particular kind of background or type of sin. Before we can intercede with power, we must ask the Lord to heal us first from relating to persons as stereotypes rather than as precious souls trapped in bondage.

REFUSING TO IMPOSE OUR NAMES ON OTHERS

We can help people grow into their new names by refusing to impose *our* names upon *them*. In small home groups, which many churches have developed, believers can find nurturing help for their Christian walks. These groups can be a great blessing, like extended families. But if the members try to impose God's directions to them on others, they can also be breeding grounds for conformity or condemnation.

God gives each of us certain directions for each season of our lives, for He alone knows our makeup, our bondages and strengths, the places that need to be made straight, the places that need to be exalted or made low. I can share what He has shown me—and I *should* share those things that will magnify His name and proclaim His faithfulness. But unless I have specifically been told by Him to pass a word along to someone else, my directions are my own and should remain my own.

As a new Bible teacher I couldn't understand why everyone in my classes didn't devote hours to reading and studying the Word. I was very frustrated because I couldn't "make" them as hungry as I was. Finally the Lord showed me that when the Israelites went out to gather manna, "some gathered more and some less," but each had just what he needed for himself and his household (Exodus 16:17). Different capacities, was the answer. Some have greater appetites in order to help feed others. By trying to force them to "gather" the way I did, I was not allowing for their own ministries.

As the Israelites prepared to go in and take the Promised Land after many years of war and homelessness, the tribes of Reuben, Gad, and Manasseh made an unusual request. Because they raised cattle, they wanted to settle in the good grazing land just outside of Canaan rather than crossing the Jordan with the rest of the tribes. At first, Moses and the leaders didn't understand, and thought they were being cowardly, not wanting to do the fighting necessary to take possession of the land. But when Reuben and Gad promised not to settle their land until they had helped the others take up their inheritance, it was agreed upon. God used them in an entirely different but strategic place, a precedent from which we can learn much.

Primarily this: that we have lives God has assigned to us, good works He has prepared for us to do, and although there are principles of Kingdom living that apply to all, we are called to different walks. The Nazirites, for example, were called not only to grow their hair long, but they were forbidden ever to taste the fruit of the vine. (They were forbidden even to eat raisins!) Jesus, on the other hand, was criticized because He and his disciples did not fast and live an outwardly ascetic lifestyle like John the Baptist's disciples did. The religious people were scandalized by His freedom. Paul, too, declared himself free in the Lord to be all things to all people, but he warned that the liberty of some was no excuse to create stumblingblocks for those called to narrower walks.

Instead of imposing our broad or narrow walk—our character and mission, our "name"—on others, we are meant to help them discern their personal direction from the Lord, hold ourselves to the Word of God as the Spirit makes application and interpretation, and then commend ourselves to God, who is the only righteous judge. *Identity is sacred ground; we dare not usurp the Lord's place as name-giver.*

SPURRING EACH OTHER TO GOOD WORKS

One of the most direct ways we can help our brothers and sisters grow into their new names is to "consider how to stir up one another to love and good works" (Hebrews 10:24). The Holy Spirit who dwells within us is an encourager; the word *parakletos* in Greek is used for the coxswain on a rowing team who uplifts his weary crew with words of praise and appreciation. If we find particular joy and help when a person shares an insight from Scripture or is articulate in counseling, if we sense a talent in someone's songs or even if we just hear a beautiful voice behind us in church, let us say so.

Many times when I have noticed the work someone has done—teaching or an administrative task, a prayer or a beautiful home—I have recalled the words *Do not withhold their wages* (Leviticus 19:13), which to me means, "Do not forget to respond to their efforts on His behalf." The Lord misses nothing that we do, and particularly precious to Him are our first feeble efforts, fearful, unpolished, full of mistakes, maybe, but pure in their intent to glorify Him.

Other times we may be called on to share our skill or experience in an area—or even constructive criticism—for we are called both to admonish and instruct (Titus 1:9, 2:3). But it would be good to pray long and hard about how and when to do this, for our enemy, the accuser, works overtime to discourage, and we must be sensitive not to crush a budding plant.

BEING WHO WE ARE

In his book *The Meaning of Persons*, Dr. Paul Tournier observes of the Lord Jesus Christ: "He alone is a person in the full meaning of the word. . . . He alone is a person without a personage (a mask)." For this reason Jesus "transforms the lives of those whom he meets, drawing out the person buried beneath the personage, and revealing personal contact to them."[3]

The only way we can truly make contact with either God or with our fellow human beings is by being truly ourselves. If we are wearing masks we imprison ourselves and block the flow of love and communion at the same time. For example, if a brother or sister comes to us in pain or discouragement or rebellion against what they think God is doing, we may be

sorely tempted to answer them through the mask of our
Christian personage, our spiritual self-image, telling ourselves that we must set good examples for them. In fact,
answers through a mask are like faint notes from a pinnacle
and are part of the very barrier that further alienates the
hurting human being before us. Our proud silence or our
automatic scriptural responses, our quick advice or theories
keep us in the superior position, far from the humble place
Jesus assumed when He dialogued with men and women. It
is only our honesty, our vulnerability, and our willingness to
understand (literally, to *stand under*) their position that will
create a climate for the wisdom and love of God to come forth
through us to them. Only when we are walking in the new
creature animated by Jesus Christ can we be free of our
masks and genuinely touch another human being.

Of his work as a Christian psychiatrist, Dr. Tournier writes
further:

> When someone lays bare to me the burning reality of his
> life, I am well aware that most of my replies could easily
> be only those of my personage. This is especially the
> case when a man expresses feelings of rebellion against
> the circumstances of his life, or his religious doubts. To
> give way to the urge to refute what he says would be to
> set up the personage of a so-called believer against that
> of a so-called unbeliever. It would be a denial of Christ's
> teaching that in the Kingdom of God the first shall be
> the last.[4]

We cannot grow into our new names in isolation. Our
identities, as individual as they are, belong also to one
corporate identity, the Body of Christ. The degree to which
you and I experience fulfillment of all that God has designed
us to be depends upon how willing our brothers and sisters
are to encourage, admonish, and set us free to be that part of
the Body. And we in turn are crucial to their development
and blossoming. Each day as we learn to accept God's design
for our lives, our identities, we must also pray for the
freedom for others to come close to their Lord and to learn
His voice. Their fulfillment is also ours.

8

RELEASING
YOUR NAME

In the first few months after I discovered that Jesus Christ was real, that He was alive, and that He was, in actuality, Lord of the Universe, I felt bathed in grace. Infused with the Holy Personality of God, I felt strange new motives of love and compassion stirring within me. Old responses such as anger and fear were conspicuous by their absence. Patience, courage, and serenity seemed boundless. I was carried along on the momentum of His energy overflowing my heart. It seemed I really was a new creature. Since I had obediently "reckoned my old self to be dead" (Romans 6:11), I foolishly figured that my transformation from utterly self-centered humanness to full-fledged sainthood was a *fait accompli*. (With a few minor areas to straighten out.)

Many Christians who share this experience refer to it as the "honeymoon period," for it parallels that sweet time in human relationships when the world narrows to just two persons. They are in love with the beautiful Lord to whom they have just surrendered their lives; and in many ways they are also in love with the new person they have glimpsed in their Lover's eyes. For a moment they have shared God's merciful perspective on themselves and have heard Him whisper their wonderful new names.

This happened in my life. I had heard my own particular new name, my unique place in His Kingdom, my true character and mission.

But for me there soon followed a period of disillusionment. Old faults and fears began to resurface, checkering my new "saintliness" with shocking evidence that my old self was not totally dead. As trials ensued the initial flush of grace seemed to peter out. Old responses came back into play.

I was sorely confused. My old self seemed like a retired fire station horse I had read about who, whenever he heard bells, dashed down the street. Was this regression a sign that I was not truly saved? I wondered. Had my saintly new heart been the product of merely another passing enthusiasm? Was the "new name" I had heard only theory and not a reality?

Fortunately the Lord sent a mature Christian teacher to me to explain what was happening, that I might not "think it strange" and lose heart. It was she who pointed me to the lives of Abraham and Jacob, Simon Peter and Paul. Early they had received the promise of new names, but it had taken a lifetime for them to *become* those names. The same was true for the nation of Israel. In God's covenant with Abraham, his descendants were promised an identity as the chosen ones of God, a nation dwelling in a "land of milk and honey," experiencing a life of fulfillment and victory. But at the time God began the work of bringing forth that identity, they were still slaves, products of a four-hundred-year heritage of helplessness. Freed from the geographical confines of Egypt, they were nonetheless enthralled by its values. Someone has observed that although it took only one night to get Israel out of Egypt, it took forty years for God to get Egypt out of them.

So, too, the new name has been given us by God. The new identity has begun to stretch its wings and make itself known. But the old self still lives. Even though it has been sentenced to death, and the ax has been laid to its root, it is not yet removed.

The Word, the promise of God, *does* become flesh, our promised names will become reality. But not overnight, as I had foolishly thought. It must be worked out; the heavenly fact must be translated into earthly reality. In George Mac-Donald's words: "As the world must be redeemed in a few men to begin with, so the soul is redeemed in a few of its thoughts, and works and ways to begin with: it takes a long time to finish the new creation of this redemption."[1]

FREEING THE NEW IDENTITY

How shall we understand the process of this redemption? It is said that the master sculptor Michelangelo often chose damaged blocks of marble that other artists had rejected. He alone could "see" the figure sleeping inside. To him, the work of chiseling and pounding, sanding and polishing, simply released the sculpture from its prison of stone. In the same way, God sees the new identity within the prison of our selves and sets to work to free the creatures He originally designed us to be. The old name must be destroyed, the new established.

But here the analogy diverges. We are not statues, passive and unconscious of our destiny. We are the living sons and daughters of the Sculptor, and He affords us the high honor or allowing us to participate in our own release. Therefore, it is imperative that we understand His purposes and recognize His methods so that we will not thwart His work in our lives.

SEEING THE OLD SELF

I submit that one of His first steps is to show us the true source of vitality and the true ugliness of that old life. What I thought was "regression" was God allowing me to see our common enemy face on, that I might ally my new self with Him and cry out for His hand to begin sculpting.

God showed Paul very clearly the tenacity of that old self. In his letter to the Roman believers, Paul described what Jeremy Taylor has called "the civil war within": "I do not understand my own actions. For I do not do what I want, but I do the very thing I hate" (Romans 7:15).

Seeing this duality and abhorring it, Paul responds by crying out to his Lord: Who will deliver me? Jesus Christ! he answers, triumphantly.

"CRUCIFIED WITH CHRIST": WHAT DOES IT MEAN?

To the Galatians Paul describes God's answer to that prayer for freedom: "I have been crucified with Christ; it is no longer I who live, but Christ who lives in me; and the life I now live in the flesh I live by faith in the Son of God, who loved me and gave himself for me" (Galatians 2:20).

Paul is expressing here not duality, but union: A miracle has taken place, the old has passed away and the new has come. He is, in essence, saying: My old self—self-creating, self-determining, self-sustaining, and self-worshiping—has been put to death! Jesus Christ has in His own body taken me to the cross with Him, and the old "I" has been dealt the death blow. The prison of self has been demolished. Yet "I," the new self, the true self, designed before the foundation of the earth, lives, he continues. Not the old Saul—enemy of Jesus Christ—but Christ-in-Paul, a new creature, centered, motivated, animated, ruled by, and infused with God Himself! And more truly *Paul* than ever. "I live now," he says, "by faith in the Son of God, who allowed His life to be pressed out that it might flow into me."

We as believers read Paul's serene declaration and we long to embrace the promise for ourselves. We rejoice over his transformation, but we stumble over what he means by the phrase *crucified with Christ*. Some of us think of it as a metaphorical expression. "Oh, yes," we nod. "In Jesus Christ, our sins have been taken to the cross. Therefore, we are entitled to a life of unmitigated blessing." We see only the fruit of Christ's death, not the need for fellowship in His death itself. In spite of logic or experience, even in spite of Scripture itself, we somehow cling to the notion that ours should be unending prosperity, health, good times, strength, victory, and protection. According to us, the figure should emerge from the stone through the ceaseless caress of a polishing cloth.

Others of us expect only the chisel: We cower in the shadow of anticipated calamity. We read this passage of Paul's and all we see is the word *crucified*. When Jesus tells us that to save our lives we must lose them, commands us to take up our crosses daily, and points us to the illustration of a grain of wheat falling to ground to die so that the new plant can come forth, all we hear are His words about death and denial. We read of refiners' fires, prunings, and purgings and trials, and we fear obliteration.

Our old self *is* being sentenced and it rightly clamors. But in the din, our spiritual ears miss the promise at the end of each pronouncement: He who loses his old life will find his new one! The broad way of ungodliness leads to death, but the narrow leads to life (literally, to broadness). I came, Jesus says, that you might have *life* abundant.

If we expect only blessing we will be alienated and confused by suffering; if we expect only suffering we will miss the joy of His encouragements. We all, then, must come into a balanced and full understanding of the work of the cross. The term *crucified* is not a theoretical one. The old self must surely die. But if to the flesh the cross is an instrument of death, it is, at the same time, the instrument of life to the new self, the key to its resurrection. Watchman Nee in his book *The Release of the Spirit* demonstrates that the new life can emerge only when the old life, the soulish, self-centered one, is broken. The alabaster jar of perfume, brought by a woman to anoint her beloved Lord, could only spread its precious fragrance when the jar itself was shattered.

With the eyes of faith, then, we must look to the cross joyfully, expectantly, for from Calvary flows the life of God Himself into all who will receive it, to awaken, reveal, strengthen, and bring to fullness the new identity He has bought for us with His blood.

To be "crucified," then, is to have the power of the cross of Jesus Christ applied to us in all of its fullness; it is to have the full panoply of God's resources poured out into each of our lives every day, chiseling away the old, shaping and polishing the new to its highest potential.

THE SCULPTOR'S METHODS

Practically speaking, God's methods are as numerous as the people He is dealing with, and they are tailor-made for each one in its appropriate season. The following illustrations are only a tiny sampling of the Sculptor's methods given so that we may have our eyes opened to see His artistry in our own lives. And that we might respond in such a way as to expedite His work.

How bravely the psalmist prays in Psalm 139.

Search me, O God, and know my heart! Try me and know my thoughts! And see if there be any wicked way in me, and lead me in the way everlasting!   verses 23–24

When we have submitted ourselves to God and long for His holiness to be formed within us, we are open for the work of revelation. And God has many ways of showing us what must be removed.

1. THE MIRROR OF THE WORD

First, last, and always, the main source of our revelation is God's Word, the Bible. It is the mirror in which we see the ways we deviate from the image of God; it is the light that reveals the impurities within us; it is the plumb line by which all other revelations must be measured. As we expose ourselves to it daily, reading the stories of God's ways, meditating on His characteristics, pondering His require-ments of our lives, we are also washed by it. For the simple procedure is that we see and we mourn and we repent, and then God cleanses us and strengthens us in righteousness. Watchman Nee says in *The Release of the Spirit* that revelation of our sin includes "both seeing and slaying."

The miraculous thing about the Word of God is its precision and pertinence. In Hebrews 4:12–13, the Word is described as

> *living and active, sharper than any two-edged sword, piercing to the division of soul and spirit, of joints and marrow, and discerning the thoughts and intentions of the heart. And before him no creature is hidden, but all are open and laid bare to the eyes of him with whom we have to do.*

"Most people," says Ellen Blackwell, an Assemblies of God minister in Virginia, "think of the Word as a giant hacksaw or a hatchet which God wields with fury, whacking off great chunks of unregenerate flesh. Actually, it is like a scalpel, by which God extricates the soul from the gross entanglements of selfishness, leaving that which is good, not to be replaced by, but animated by the Spirit, as it was in the beginning. God delicately excises things which are bound and which are not allowed their full life. It is the work of the Lord to free the riches of the soul—not to kill it off—so that each personality can become what it is supposed to be."

In the story of the conversion of St. Augustine the Word is miraculous in its ability to pierce to the heart of the need within a person. Augustine had lived a life away from his childhood faith, and at thirty-two had tasted deeply of many heresies as well as promiscuous self-indulgence. Unable to escape his guilt, he cried out to God, "Why not is there this hour an end to my uncleanness?"

> Lo! I heard from a neighbouring house a voice, as of boy or girl, I know not, chanting, and oft repeating, "Take up and read; Take up and read." Instantly, my counte-nance altered, I began to think most intently whether children were wont in any kind of play to sing such words: nor could I remember ever to have heard the like. So checking the torrent of my tears, I arose; interpreting it to be no other than a command from God to open the book, and read the first chapter I should find. . . . I seized, opened, and in silence read that section on which my eyes first fell: Not in rioting and drunkenness, not in chambering and wantonness, not in strife and envying; but put ye on the Lord Jesus Christ, and make not provision for the flesh, in concu-piscence. No further would I read; nor needed I: for instantly, at the end of this sentence, by a light as it were of serenity infused into my heart, all the darkness of doubt vanished away.[2]

THE STILL, SMALL VOICE

The Lord speaks to us daily within the chambers of our own hearts. One morning in my prayer time I was feeling very dry spiritually. I was dutifully doing devotions, going to church, even teaching a Bible study, but my heart just wasn't in it. I was not even really asking the Lord what was going on, but He spoke to me anyway, just one word: *Hypocrite*. It was spoken lovingly, gently, almost humorously, not the way He had said it to the scribes and Pharisees (Matthew 23:13, *et al*). He was saying it in its original meaning: "mask." In one word he conveyed to me the whole problem: I had fallen into acting spiritual—playing Mrs. Christian. I was doing my old imitation of a Christian rather than letting things flow from my relationship with Him. No wonder I had run out of fuel.

Another time I awoke with the word *stridor* in my mind. When I looked it up in the dictionary and learned that it meant a "harshness of voice," I knew He was calling for me to repent of the sarcasm that had crept back into my speech. He had given me a promise: "If you utter what is precious and not what is worthless, you shall be as my mouth" (Jeremiah 15:19), but my conversation was becoming harsh and strident, so I had to reconsecrate to Him my mouth and my thoughts.

DREAMS

As we have previously seen, the Lord can use dreams to guide and direct us. He can also use them to show us areas that need repentance and healing. Morton Kelsey, John Sanford, and others have written extensively on the ways the Lord uses dreams to show us those parts of ourselves that we otherwise might never see. In my own life the Lord often gives me such glimpses that usually guide me to His Word for specifics.

For example, in one bizarre dream He showed me a real spiritual danger. In the dream I was a prostitute awakening from some liaison. As I began to dress, I found that my skirt was reversible: flowered and gaily colored on one side, black on the other. Pondering the dream's main theme of adultery, I let the word *skirt* guide me through Scripture to Lamentations 1:9, a vivid description of the spiritual adultery of Jerusalem: "Her uncleanness was in her skirts; she took no thought of her doom; therefore her fall is terrible."

I asked the Lord to show me in what way I was being unfaithful. He led me to the fourth chapter of John, the story of the woman at the well, which I read until something "lit up." In verse 28, as the woman went away into the city to tell the people that she had found the Messiah (the Living Water), the Scripture says she "left her water jar." The Lord showed me that I was to leave my "jar," that is, my dependence on my own devices for teaching and evangeliz-

ing, and that I could choose *His* words, which would carry
life (the flowered skirt), or *my* words, which no matter how
clever would be lifeless (the black skirt). He was calling for
complete fidelity in my relationship with Him.

CIRCUMSTANCES

Not only God's Word but His arrangement of circumstances can bring us to see the weaknesses and dross within
us.

My mother, who seemed to be one of the Lord's most
active servants, a Martha as well as a Mary, one day found
herself in the hospital with assorted injuries. Her car had
been broadsided. "Lord," she cried out, "it says in Psalm 91
that no accidents shall befall Your saints." The Lord answered her, "Marjorie, what makes you think this was an
accident?" During her time in the hospital she learned how
difficult it was for her to accept ministry from others. She had
been busy and happy in the role of foot-washer; to experience
weakness and dependence on the help of others was a great
blow to the pride she never suspected lay in her heart.
Because she was an eager, teachable disciple, my mother
forever after counted that one of the most valuable experiences of her life.

"Fiery trials" usually makes us think of catastrophe and
loss: deaths of loved ones, loss of home or property, or
chronic illnesses. Sometimes it's not anything as major as
that. An hour stuck in rush-hour traffic with shrieking
children in the back of the station wagon and the needle
edging "E" reveals to me angers, impatience, indignation,
fears, unbelief, and even ethnic prejudices I never knew were
there! If we have the ears to hear, practically any situation
can be used to show us this. We may have a rough time at
our work places surrounded by apathy or cutthroat ambition,
by inefficiency, waste, and partiality. We may have a job that
is unfulfilling, almost meaningless, or at home we may find
the work maintaining a house maddeningly monotonous. In

the "furnace" of tedium and frustration, things will surface that might never have shown themselves. Deep reservoirs of impatience, anger, resentment, self-pity, may lurk below the surface, and need to be handed over to the Lord for disposal.

PEOPLE

The Lord can and does use people to reveal our need for repentance. A rebellious child, an uncommunicative spouse, a tactless neighbor, a friend whose seemingly perfect competence shows us our complete inadequacy, a co-worker whose sarcasm makes us uncomfortable, a relative who ridicules us for our "religious fanaticism" all can be revealing, for Scripture tells us that the things that annoy us most are the very things we dislike in ourselves. All of us who are parents have probably had the humbling experience of finding our own worst traits, our greed or petulance, in the transparency of our children. In fact, Jesus tells us that judging is a dangerous game for this reason: The speck we see in our brother's eye (and are so anxious to comment on) is, in fact, simply the reflection of the log that is stuck in our eye.

We had spent all day cleaning house for a new believer who was going through a difficult third pregnancy. She was having trouble believing that God really knew and cared about her problem. So we sought to prove it through Windex and fellowship. As she lay on the sofa, we bustled about, doing more housecleaning in one day than I had done in a year at my house. As we were leaving, I asked: *"Now* do you believe that the Lord loves you?" "I guess so," she whined. I was puffing up with indignation, thinking of the sliding glass doors I had just polished, when to my surprise I seemed to see my own face superimposed on hers. *How many times have you resisted the evidence of My love for you?* the Lord smiled. Touché.

When we allow God to show us ourselves clearly, we will be convinced that, as Jeremiah says, "The heart is deceitful

above all things, and desperately corrupt; who can understand it?" (Jeremiah 17:9). Only the Lord, who will show us.
Paul understood this truth and vowed: "I do not even judge
myself. I am not aware of anything against myself, but I am
not thereby acquitted. It is the Lord who judges me" (1
Corinthians 4:3–4). We must leave it to the convicting power
of the Holy Spirit, for He alone can see into our hearts and
read their true complexions.

REMOVING THE OLD SELF

Larry Tomczak has commented, "The Lord doesn't want to
wound your pride. . . . He wants to kill it!" But when we
hear of the Lord wanting to eradicate our pride, we may fear
that He will humiliate us to do so. To crush our pride He may
crush and obliterate *us*, we fear. We must remember that God
has sworn vengeance, not on us, His creatures, but on the
old self, the prison that holds us back from being all He
wants us to be. God can humble us without humiliating us if
we come to Him repentant, anxious to be set free.

REMOVING THE OLD SELF BY BLESSING

Many times the very way He will use—for "His ways are
not our ways" (Isaiah 55:9)—is by blessing us. Remember
how Jesus caused the school of fish to come into Peter's net?
It caused a mighty spirit of repentance to come over the
skeptical Peter.

The Scripture tells us that God's kindness is meant to do
exactly that: to lead us to repentance (Romans 2:4) and the
psalmist observes that it is because He forgives us that we
reverence Him (Psalm 130:4). God knows that often mercy is
the very thing that will most effectively humble our hearts.

Being childless for many years, I had nearly grown proud
in my "martyrdom," almost feeling a perverse kind of
strength in doing without the blessing that so many women

around me took for granted. The way the Lord destroyed that pride was to send us the desire of our hearts—a lovely baby. No longer could I court martyrdom. With that blessing God healed me not only in body but in spirit and soul. He has further blessed us with a second daughter, causing a profound humbling in the face of His goodness.

Another experience showed me again how effective is God's kindness. Before I was a Christian I had left a job because of a deep clash with my boss. His lifestyle and his values repelled me, and when I had resigned, I had left without really talking things over. When I became a believer I was convicted of my need for some kind of reconciliation with him, but I didn't know quite what to do. I prayed and asked the Lord to somehow heal the breach. In my own scenario I saw myself in a situation where he would desperately need my help and I would have a chance to show him my new self by my response.

But God had another idea entirely. One day, as Michael and I were driving away from his office, our car stopped dead in the middle of a one-way street in downtown Washington, D.C. The motor wouldn't even do us the courtesy of turning over, and it was so late that there were no people around to help. We were both getting pretty angry as Michael got in and out of the car, glaring helplessly under the hood. To my chagrin I spotted coming down the street toward us my old boss. He called cheerfully to us, telling us he would be right back with his car. As we awaited his return I agonized: Why had God done this to me? How would I break the ice?

As we climbed into his car, I got into the backseat in silence, still fumbling, feeling humiliated at being at his mercy. How in the world could I possibly think of something conciliatory to say to him? My heart was still hard toward him.

Then my eye fell on something on the backseat: a sales receipt from a local nursery. I remembered how he had spoken one day of planting daffodils and about how much he loved them. Suddenly my heart, which had hardened with guilt, was broken open at the thought of this man on his knees working in his yard, planting flowers. As I managed to ask how his garden was doing, I felt the love of God flowing toward him through me, healing those cold proud places in me as well.

REMOVING THE OLD SELF BY HUMOR

Sometimes the Lord deals humorously with us. Nancy, a dear friend who grew up in a very orthodox and old-fashioned Catholic home, was raised on stories of persecuted saints and movies about peasant girls constantly suffering for the glory of God. Nancy even put pebbles in her shoes for the walk to school so that God would be pleased with her, too. When she came to know Him in a personal way, she put much of her tendency to martyrdom behind her as religiosity. But a residue remained, tempting her to be self-pitying and resentful, especially toward her husband whom she regarded as a "hard taskmaster" because he expected their home to be spick-and-span at all times.

One night near midnight when the kids had gone to bed, she was on her knees scrubbing away on the kitchen floor, outwardly submissive but inwardly seething. All of a sudden, she told me, she looked up to see a vision that healed her of her last tendency toward martyrdom. She saw in her mind's eye the Lord laughing. "*Song of Bernadette*, right?" was all He had to say.

I had a similar experience with God's healing humor. When I was in college I was given a beautiful beaver coat by an older friend. It was dark brown, heavy and warm; inside the satin lining her initials were embroidered in elaborate script. I loved the coat, but I was opposed to wearing fur, so for many years I carted it around from dorm to apartment. I never wore it, but I couldn't bear to throw it away! Then I became a Christian and I read in Luke 3:11, "He who has two coats, let him share with him who has none."

In obedience I took the coat to a local church-run thrift

shop. To my surprise, it was hard to part with, but I envisioned a poor old woman shuffling along through howling winds and snowdrifts, toasty warm in my beaver coat, praising God for my generosity. I never knew how proud I was of my "philanthropy" until one evening several months later. As it happened, I was in our local library looking up stories for a church presentation on "Protestant saints." Kneeling to look on the bottom shelf, I glanced through the stacks at the tables and chairs just beyond it.

A dark brown beaver coat was flung over the back of one of the chairs. I squinted with astonishment. The satin-stitched initials were the same! It was *my* coat! My heart pounded as I thanked the Lord that I was going to have a chance to see *my* poor old lady.

Crouched in the stacks, I watched in horror as a frosted blonde in gray wool slacks and an expensive silk blouse strolled over and retrieved her coat.

I had forgotten that the thrift shop was open to all, even wealthy bargain hunters. "Lord!" I cried out in protest. He answered: "You gave the coat for My sake, didn't you? It was the giving that was important." Lady Bountiful never rode quite as high again.

REMOVING THE OLD SELF THROUGH UNRAVELING OUR SELF-RELIANCE

Our old self thrives on the illusion that it can do without God. In fact, Satan's lure to Eve was that if she ate of the fruit of the Tree of the Knowledge of Good and Evil, she could discern good and evil for herself, like God, and could function independent of Him. Therefore, God has to come against self-reliance. Jacob's hip had to be put out of joint to keep him close to God, His Creator and Sustainer. Jesus says, "Apart from Me you can do nothing," but we don't really believe that until He allows it to be demonstrated in our lives, and we find our own competence beginning to fail us.

In Deuteronomy 8:2–10, Moses reveals Yahweh's motives in deliberately leading the Israelites into the wilderness:

> *You shall remember all the way which the Lord your God has led you these forty years in the wilderness, that he might humble you, testing you to know what was in your heart, whether you would keep his commandments, or not. And he humbled you and let you hunger and fed you with manna, which you did not know, nor did your fathers know; that he might make you know that man does not live by bread alone, but that man lives by everything that proceeds out of the mouth of the Lord. Your clothing did not wear out upon you, and your foot did not swell, these forty years. Know then in your heart that, as a man disciplines his son, the Lord your God disciplines you.*

God allowed the resources of the Israelites to fail them (the bread they had brought from Egypt ran out, the water they found was undrinkable) so that He could demonstrate His miraculous power and faithfulness. And so He still works. Many of us have experienced the strange process of finding our strength retracted, withdrawn, failing us. The first formal teaching I gave lasted somewhere near an hour, and when it was done, someone asked if I wanted a glass of water. To my surprise, I couldn't find the words to say, "Yes, I do." My mind was a blank. It only lasted a second, but in it I realized that words, and a mouth that could speak them, were a sovereign gift, and that apart from Him I truly could "do nothing."

In many other people's lives I have seen God work by unraveling self-reliance. Linda, whose forte is organizing people and programs, once worked as a career counselor, testing and helping people recognize their own particular skills and interests. After she became a believer to her horror, she began to lose her ability to make quick and incisive analyses. It returned only when she prayed for God's insights and guidance in working with people. As she has hungered for help, He has replaced her old "bread" with supernatural manna—wisdom from above. She has since entered the Episcopal priesthood and finds that this lesson in trusting in the Lord rather than leaning on her own understanding (Proverbs 3:5) holds her in good stead.

My sister-in-law Terry, a creative cook and multi-talented person, was accustomed to success in almost everything she tackled. It was a major defeat to her patient perseverance when she spent an entire afternoon trying to get one pie crust rolled out right. The frustration and anger she discovered while wrestling with the pie crust showed her the degree to which she relied on her own skill. God had begun the process of weaning her from self-reliance and into a new way of walking with Him.

John and Paula Sandford have observed that many Christian psychologists and counselors work in the wrong direction: patching people up toward the goal of perfection. "Psychologists would mend our self-images so that we could have confidence in ourselves. Christ would slay all our fleshly self-confidence so that our only self-image becomes: I can do all things *through Christ* who strengthens me" (Philippians 4:13).[3] Paul Tournier agrees:

> To experience the "new birth" of which our Lord speaks (John 3:3), to become the "new man" of which St. Paul speaks (Ephesians 4:24), is indeed to become adult, to attain to the fullness of humanity ordained by God, but it is much more than that. It is to recover, through the redemption of Christ, fellowship with God and *dependence on Him*.[4]

THE ROLE OF TRIALS

In addition to removing the dross, God is also at work to establish, cultivate, and strengthen the new name within us, that identity that is born of His Spirit. This new self must be shaped and equipped with God's characteristics for the life it now lives.

STRETCHING OUR FAITH

For example, one of God's main goals is to stretch our faith, for without faith it is impossible to please Him (Hebrews 11:6). We find an example of His methods in Matthew 15:22–28:

> *And behold, a Canaanite woman from that region came out and cried, "Have mercy on me, O Lord, Son of David; my daughter is severely possessed by a demon." But he did not answer her a word. And his disciples came and begged him, saying, "Send her away, for she is crying after us." He answered, "I was sent only to the lost sheep of the house of Israel." But she came and knelt before him, saying, "Lord, help me." And he answered, "It is not fair to take the children's bread and throw it to the dogs." She said, "Yes, Lord, yet even the dogs eat the crumbs that fall from their master's table." Then Jesus answered her, "O woman, great is your faith! Be it done for you as you desire." And her daughter was healed instantly.*

This woman was not of the chosen race of Israel, but a Gentile, hence Jesus' use of the epithet *dog*. However, it is obvious that she knew who He was and believed in Him. At first, Jesus didn't even answer her. Then He put her off by saying that He hadn't been sent to her people, only the Israelites. But she would not be dissuaded; her need was too great and her pride, challenged by His protests, died. She didn't even take umbrage at being called a dog. By that point her faith was so strong and so focused on Him as the only answer, that Jesus saw in her a conduit through which to pour His healing power upon the possessed daughter far away. And He commended her publicly.

In this story is telescoped the ways the Lord works in our lives. First, He seems not to answer us at all; then it seems we receive a no, all of which forces us to become more zealous in our prayer, more pure. In James 4:2–3 we are told, "You do not have, because you do not ask. You ask and do not receive, because you ask wrongly, to spend it on your passions." God's silence stretches out our faith; His negative answers can teach us how to pray with greater purity of heart by purging us of our selfish concerns and bringing us closer to His will. They also teach us to wait and listen with sharper hearing.

BUILDING OUR PATIENCE

Someone has said that the devil's middle name is "speed." His goals are temporal, his methods expedient. And what he produces in human hearts is a fretting, fearful kind of urgency and anxiety. God, who abides in eternity, can afford to take His time because Love outlasts all things, He can afford to be patient, and He desires to impart this divine characteristic to His people. James describes God's method of working into us this precious virtue:

> Count it all joy, my brethren, when you meet various trials, for you know that the testing of your faith produces steadfastness [patience]. And let steadfastness have its full effect, that you may be perfect and complete, lacking in nothing.   James 1:2–4

Trials and testing, enduring, waiting, these are the only ways of attaining patience. But James also tells us that we might as well consider all our trying experiences as joy, for that is what they will produce in our lives—an attitude of joyful patience that will make us mature, able to remain peaceful no matter what happens.

I have always thought of God's teaching through constant trial as being similar to the muscle-building technique of isometrics. A little pressure over a long time builds muscles just as strong as the weightlifting jerk-and-press methods, which are so dramatic to watch. And the race set before Christians is more often a marathon than a sprint; therefore, the Lord strives to teach His people to wait.

Abram had to wait twenty-five years for the fulfillment of the promise of a son. Jacob waited for Rachel. Joseph waited for vindication. Moses waited forty years to free his people.

The Israelites as a nation waited 430 years for their deliverance from bondage in Egypt. Even Jesus had to wait for His main mission on earth to begin (Luke 12:50): "I have a baptism to be baptized with; and how I am constrained [pressed in] until it is accomplished!"

But when James speaks of our "testing" through trials, we must not bring to this word our childish experience of tests in school, where we were convinced that the teacher's motives were to flunk us. When God allows illness or obstacles, or causes us to wait in other ways for the things we desire, His purpose is never that we should fall away in despair and give up; His purpose is to strengthen *through just the right amount of stress* our capacity to hang on by faith, so that we will be there for the larger answer He has for us. He wants us to learn to draw on His infinite resource of patience.

INCREASING OUR CAPACITY FOR WARFARE

It is in the furnace of everyday trials and obstacles that we find our new selves tempered for battle. The Christian life is one of warfare, for the enemy's sole occupation is to try to thwart the purposes of God by attacking His people. Therefore, God would not have us ignorant or weak. We are filled with His Spirit, but we learn to use the weapons of our warfare (the Word and prayer) and that cannot be done in a vacuum; they must be employed, for our skill to grow.

When the Israelites left Egypt the Bible says specifically that they were "equipped for battle" (Exodus 13:18). In other words, they must have possessed weapons and supplies. But God led them into the wilderness first. There they learned the miraculous nature and fidelity of God's provision (such as water from the rock and the manna) and could trust God enough to fight His way rather than the world's. When they were ready, God finally permitted them to "see war" (Exodus 17). Led by Joshua and supported in prayer by Moses, Aaron, and Hur, they routed the ambushing Amalekites.

Like the Israelites we must be exposed to battle if we would learn to fight. Therefore, God allows the enemy to parade his tactics—harassments, interruptions, distractions, oppressions—every day. He allows this so that we can learn to recognize and defeat the enemy in the authority of the name of the Lord Jesus Christ.

DEVELOPING OUR INDIVIDUAL GIFTS

A few years ago a book called *The Peter Principle* changed the way America looked at management policies and added a phrase to popular vocabulary. The "Peter Principle" is the paradoxical practice of promoting a person out of his or her field of competency and into a place for which he or she has no skill, creating a whole hierarchy of incompetents. Obviously, in the secular world this is not good practice.

Yet in the Kingdom of God, the Lord operates in just such a way, a way we may also call the "Peter Principle." That is His method of calling us as He did Peter out of our "boats," our places of competence, safety, complacency, and into realms for which we are not naturally equipped. He calls us up higher, out of the place where we can rely on our own experience or lean on our own understanding and into places where we must embrace Him, we must keep our eyes unswervingly on Him, or like Peter, we will drown. If we experience frustration with the work we're doing or the ministry we're engaged in, it may be that this is God's way of calling us higher.

Like the Israelites who had to be extruded from Egypt, we are conservative creatures, afraid of change, afraid of greatness, but God has contracted to bring us into all He designed us to be, and He will get us there, whether we like it or not. C. S. Lewis observed in *Mere Christianity*:

Imagine yourself as a living house. God comes in to rebuild that house. At first, perhaps, you can understand what He is doing. He is getting the drains right and stopping the leaks in the roof and so on; you knew that those jobs needed doing and so you are not surprised. But presently he starts knocking the house about in a way that hurts abominably and does not seem to make sense. What on earth is he up to? The explanation is that he is building quite a different house from the one you thought of—throwing out a new wing here, putting on an extra floor there, running up towers, making courtyards. You thought you were going to be made into a decent little cottage; but he is building a palace.[5]

Trials are God's tools. Paul's imprisonment must have caused him anguish for not being able to freely preach the Gospel in person, yet the fact that he was forced to write down his revelations from the Lord made them available to all those who would follow Jesus in the centuries to come. Amy Carmichael's chronic illness forced her into a life of contemplation, prayer, and writing that has similarly blessed the Body of Christ. Joni Eareckson's tragic accident that left her a quadriplegic gave her a worldwide ministry to those who suffer physical or mental limitation. And Catherine Marshall's abundant career as a writer and teacher began at the death of her husband Peter and her attempt to edit his sermons.

Sometimes our ministries and gifts must all be passed through the fire, lest they become the focus of our life rather than the Giver, and God must bring things into our lives to keep us mindful that we are stewards of *His* ministry. He can raise up rocks to praise Him; He can make a donkey preach a sermon, employ a whale in evangelism, and cause the sun itself to stand still to fulfill His purposes. He does us an honor by entrusting us with the jobs He has for each one of us. What we must remember is that as God, like the mother eagle, flings us from the nest, so too He soars beneath so we will never fall.

PRODUCING HIS IMAGE

God's main purpose is to produce His image in each one of us. Paul E. Billheimer in *Don't Waste Your Sorrows* explains why that transformation requires suffering. Because believers are destined to reign with Christ in the world to come, he writes, God must work in this world to make our hearts and minds like His. The nature of our fallen hearts is to be self-centered; thus, their transformation into totally other-directed hearts (like the Lord's) is painful. We only come into self-sacrificial, compassionate (divine) love by tasting, as Jesus did, pain, frustration, loss, and sorrow.

Scripture confirms that truth: If we would fellowship with Jesus Christ in glory, we must also taste His suffering. Peter writes:

> *Beloved, do not be surprised at the fiery ordeal which comes upon you to prove you, as though something strange were happening to you. But rejoice in so far as you share Christ's sufferings, that you may also rejoice and be glad when his glory is revealed.* 1 Peter 4:12–13

Paul contends that the extent to which we share His suffering is the extent to which we will share in the power of His resurrection. Tragedies, unhappy relationships, slander, misunderstanding, reviling, neglect, insults, annoyances—all these things, if we will not "waste" them but will let them drive us closer to God—will teach us how to endure in His power, and to reign in His wisdom and love.

In this life trials can equip us to minister as He would. Paul writes of the way we are prepared to know and show Christ's loving mercy and healing:

> *Blessed be the God and Father of our Lord Jesus Christ, the Father of mercies and God of all comfort, who comforts us in all our affliction, so that we may be able to comfort those who are in affliction, with the comfort with which we ourselves are comforted by God.*
> 2 Corinthians 1:3–4

If suffering is an inescapable fact of transformation, we are not left to go through it alone. Isaiah says of the Lord and His people that "in all their affliction he was afflicted" (Isaiah

63:9) for "he does not willingly grieve the sons of men"
(Lamentations 3:33). And He teaches our brothers and sisters
to be with us, too, to bear our burdens (Galatians 6:2).

Karen Burton Mains in *Open Heart—Open Home* tells of a
period of many months when she had been under great
stress. Her father and mother had both been seriously ill, her
three-year-old had been hit by a bicycle, an older child had
been injured, and the others had had scarlet fever and throat
and ear infections. Her washer, the dryer, the freezer had all
gone haywire, as had the kitchen faucet and the muffler on
the car. Then she herself came down with the strength-
draining disease, mononucleosis.

> I fought the despairing "whys." I felt like a little child
> who had been spanked again and again for some
> unknown error. I was willing to change my unruly
> behavior but I didn't know what I was doing wrong.
> One afternoon Mother came with food. The last thing
> she needed was to care for me. "Do you have this awful
> feeling that someone somewhere doesn't like us?" I
> ventured timidly, afraid to reveal my stricken feelings.
> "No," she replied softly. "I have a feeling that Some-
> one somewhere knows we won't be the people He
> wants us to be without pain. Don't ask where God's
> love is. This is His shadow side. It is here in these bad
> things." Laying her hands on me, she prayed for
> healing. My chastened soul found comfort and the
> wounds began to heal.[6]

GOD'S METHODS ARE TAILOR-MADE

Whatever methods God uses, each is selected according to
individual need. My husband and I discovered this when,
shortly after we became Christians, the Lord convicted us
that we must stop smoking for we were both deeply addicted.
I went cold turkey, and the first week or so was hellish. As a
writer I was into a familiar rhythm of writing, stopping,
lighting up, thinking, and typing again. I feared I'd never be

able to work again. But God was good, and He gave me inch by inch the grace I needed to kick the habit. Michael tried that method, too, but without success. Then, one morning as he stood at the bus stop, he heard a voice saying, "You don't need those anymore." He threw away a freshly opened pack and never really craved another cigarette again.

I went to the Lord: Hadn't I had sufficient faith? Had I forgotten to ask for a simple miracle? His answer to me came several months later when I could see it clearly. Michael knew his own willpower, his own strength; he needed a miracle in order to see God's sovereign power to deliver and set free. I needed to know that through God I could do something excruciatingly hard and still come out victorious. He gave us both what we will most value in the years to come.

God's methods of removing the dross and strengthening the good are also in exact proportion to the need. Many times we fear great calamity, for those are the methods that are written about in dramatic testimonies. But God allays our fears through the prophet Isaiah by directing us to consider a wise farmer: He

> is instructed aright; his God teaches him. Dill is not threshed with a threshing sledge nor is a cart wheel rolled over cummin; but dill is beaten out with a stick, and cummin with a rod. Does one crush bread grain? No, he does not thresh it for ever; when he drives his cart wheel over it with his horses he does not crush it. This also comes from the Lord of hosts; he is wonderful in counsel, and excellent in wisdom.　　　　　　　　　　　　　　　　　　　Isaiah 28:26–29

God, who teaches the farmer appropriate methods to prepare his grain, will not bring inappropriate measures upon our lives.

In addition He reminds us, "For I know the plans I have for you, plans for welfare and not for evil, to give you a future and a hope" (Jeremiah 29:11). He is not willing that any should perish but instead wants us equipped to walk in the fullness of our identities and His blessing. When trial and stress and need are permitted to come into our lives we must remember that they are first weighed with divine wisdom and love. The hand that places them in our path is the same hand pierced by the cross at Calvary, the hand that has our names engraved upon its palm (Isaiah 49:16). All that comes our way comes filtered through the great love that kept our Savior upon that cross.

Our response is up to us. We can choose to turn away, to resist our crosses, or we can embrace them as the instruments of a loving and solicitous teacher to bring us into conformity with His image. We marvel at the story of Job, a man devoted enough to God that in the day when all his blessings—family, wealth, health—were taken from him, he could say with conviction, "The Lord has given and the Lord has taken away. Blessed be the name of the Lord." But it is interesting to note that the name *Job* can be translated either "hostile" or "penitent." What a revealing truth! The sufferings and losses and pain could have made Job bitter and resentful, hurling him into total rebellion against the Lord. Instead, because he clung to God through *all* circumstances, he was permitted to see God face to face. And then he received greater blessing than at first.

May our prayer be that our trials as well as our blessings will work God's perfect and loving purpose in our lives: the full manifestation of our new names.

9

FOR HIS NAME'S SAKE

St. Augustine urged: "Seek for yourself, O man; search for your true self. He who seeks shall find himself in God." C. S. Lewis, however, once defined hell as "the ruthless, sleepless, unsmiling concentration upon self." Is the pursuit of our "names" a path to deeper communion with God? Or is it a snare? Are we simply putting a religious face on a worldly pursuit? Satan would have us believe the latter.

Satan would have us twist Jesus' message into a perverse kind of self-denial. He would take Jesus' commands—such as "If you would find your life, lose it," and "If you would be my disciple, deny yourself"—and turn them into false piety, the kind that has "an appearance of wisdom . . . in promoting rigor of devotion and self-abasement" (Colossians 2:23) but which actually focuses us more frantically than ever on ourselves. He would have us denigrate ourselves to ourselves, failing to appreciate our worth in the sight of the God who loved us enough to give His very own Son for us, and repressing the unique things God has put within us. Unconscious of God's work and His purpose in our lives, we would toil our years away, trying in vain to achieve our own "holiness."

God, on the other hand, calls for us time and time again to come into the fullness of redemption that He has for us. Scripture is filled with exhortations to God's people to receive His blessings and to let the world know it. The psalmist cries out, "Let the redeemed of the Lord say so!" (Psalm 107:2) and Jeremiah invites, "The Lord has brought forth our vindication; come, let us declare in Zion the works of the Lord our God" (Jeremiah 51:10). Jesus commands one man: " 'Return to your home, and declare how much God has done for you.' And he went away, proclaiming throughout the whole city how much Jesus had done for him" (Luke 8:39). And again, David exalts: "All thy works shall give thanks to thee, O Lord, and all thy saints shall bless thee! They shall speak of the glory of thy kingdom, and tell of thy power" (Psalm 145:10–11).

JEWELS IN HIS CROWN

We pursue our new identities, first of all, because our redemption was the ultimate mission of Jesus Christ. When Jesus went to the cross to die, we are told in Hebrews 2:12 that though He despised the shame of a criminal's execution, He was able to go through with it "for the joy that was set before Him." A prophetic word about the aftermath of the cross (Isaiah 53:11) says the same: "He shall see the fruit of the travail of his soul and be satisfied." What is that joy and fruit of the cross? Is it merely our forgiveness, as wonderful a gift as that is? If we read all He says to us in His Word, surely we cannot believe that. The Israelites were not merely saved *from* Egypt; they were saved *for* the Promised Land. So, too, we are not merely saved *from* hell, slated to wander in some neutral state till "the sweet bye and bye" when we finally enter heaven.

No, as David declares in Psalm 27:13: "I believe that I shall see the goodness of the Lord in the land of the living!" Jesus Christ came to suffer and to die that we might share in His resurrection life not just in ages to come but here and now. He came "to bring many sons to glory" (Hebrews 2:10) and "to present us faultless before the presence of his glory with exceeding joy" (Jude 24). Glory, as the term is used in Scripture, means the fruition of something; therefore, we can understand that Jesus' ultimate goal was to set us free to blossom into maturity, into the creatures God designed us to be, in the beginning. This is the "fruit" of the travail of His soul.

Jesus' redemptive work does not simply make us righteous in a legal sense before God: It makes us *right*. In the poetry of prophetic utterance:

> *Then the eyes of the blind shall be opened, and the ears of the deaf unstopped; then shall the lame man leap like a hart, and the tongue of the dumb sing for joy, For waters shall break forth in the wilderness, and streams in the desert; the burning sand shall become a pool, and the thirsty ground springs of water.*   Isaiah 35:5–6

What has been twisted and blasted by our sinfulness and by the devices of the enemy He will surely restore.

God wants us to enter the fullness of our new identities because our wholeness brings glory to Jesus Christ. We are told that when Jesus went to Calvary, the angels were puzzled (1 Peter 1:12): not having fallen from grace themselves, they didn't understand the need for redemption. Neither could they fathom the great love in the heart of the Rescuer for these rebellious humans. In the words of the old hymn, they must have asked, "What wondrous love is this?" But Jesus Himself tells us that, understanding it or not, those same angels, upon seeing the salvation of a single sinner, break forth throughout heaven in mighty shouts of praise to the Redeemer who wrought that deliverance (Luke 15:7).

In Isaiah 43:7, the Lord speaks of those who are called by His name and says explicitly that they have been created for His glory. According to 1 Peter 2:9 we have been transferred from the kingdom of darkness into His "marvelous light" for the same purpose: "that we might declare the wonderful deeds" of the Lord. In heaven we are regarded as His "spoils," His trophies of war, as it were. In fact, He speaks of us as a royal diadem in His hand (Isaiah 62:3) and as His "jewels" (Malachi 3:17).

Therefore, we have a responsibility. If we are His jewels, His trophies of war, we must pray: Make me all that You intended me to be. Give me a holy ambition to be as much like You as I can possibly be. Give me an insatiable hunger and thirst to live in the righteousness You have designed into me. Create in me a continuing desire to find my true identity in You and in Your service, so that You might be praised and honored for what You have accomplished. Make me a fit reflection of Your loveliness, that it might bring glory to You among all the hosts of heaven and among all the creatures of Your universe.

We must pray, in other words, to come into the fullness of our new names!

CHOOSING TO LOSE

But still, our new identity is not just for our sakes. We have a responsibility to "find" ourselves so that we then might deliberately lose ourselves in service to others, as He did. As we have seen:

Jesus, knowing that the Father had given all things into his hands, and that he had come from God and was going to God, rose from supper, laid aside his garments, and girded himself with a towel. Then he poured water into a basin, and began to wash the disciples' feet, and to wipe them with the towel with which he was girded.

John 13:3–5

The story continues in verses 12–15:

When he had washed their feet, and taken his garments, and resumed his place, he said to them, "Do you know what I have done to you? You call me Teacher and Lord; and you are right, for so I am. If I then, your Lord and Teacher, have washed your feet, you also ought to wash one another's feet, for I have given you an example, that you also should do as I have done to you."

We are told to do what Jesus has done, and I believe it is no accident that in this same passage we are given a glimpse into His interior thought: There is a link between His self-knowledge, His security in His identity, and His ability to make Himself the lowest of servants performing the most menial of tasks. What is the secret to Jesus' divine humility, His full concentration on others? What is at the heart of His total clear-sighted focus on *their* needs, and not His own, even in the hour before He faces the agony of Gethsemane? We see the answer in those very first verses: Jesus' identity was settled. "Knowing that the Father had given all things into His hands, and that He had come from God and was going to God, He knelt. . . ." He knew exactly who He was; He knew where He was going.

So now we are coming full circle. As long as we humans are unsure of who we are, where we have come from, and where we are going, we will be seeking to create by our own devices a name for ourselves, our invented identities. We will continue to be like gerbils on a wheel, consumed by that search. As long as that question "Who am I?" remains unanswered (and it *will* be, if we look anywhere but to God Himself for it), then we will never be free to truly put another before ourselves. We may spend our money, time, and energy in philanthropic frenzies, we may "give up our bodies to be burned" in zealous causes (1 Corinthians 13:3) but it will profit us nothing.

When we, however, rest in what Christ will make of us, when we are convinced that our names will be "wonderful," too, in short, when we know who He is, and that we, too, have come from Him and are going to Him, then and only then the clamor of our egocentricity will be stilled. Then we can simply live, trusting and following Him, serving others even as He served.

Then and only then we can lay down our self-made Christian identities with their good works, their strivings after righteousness, and their posturings, and live in that unself-consciousness Jesus described in His Sermon on the Mount: "Do not let your left hand know what your right hand is doing" (Matthew 6:3).

Jesus is speaking here of almsgiving, telling us that if we are moving in the power of the Holy Spirit, our good works will flow in the natural, automatic way our feet relate to each other in the act of walking. After infancy most of us rarely have to think and analyze our walking—it occurs as a natural outflowing movement of our bodies. When we are surrendered to Him, we can serve in that same kind of total unself-consciousness.

Keith Miller in his book *The Becomers* observes that only those people "whose sanity, security, and worth are founded on their continuing relation to God and each other are not 'too busy' with their own kingdoms to be God's people in the world." This kind of unself-conscious service, that simply *does*, without scrutinizing all the ramifications of its own righteousness, is commended by our Lord in Matthew 25, when He calls His true followers to Himself at the end of the world and says to them:

> *I was hungry and you gave me food, I was thirsty and you gave me drink, I was a stranger and you welcomed me, I was naked and you clothed me, I was sick and you visited me, I was in prison and you came to me.*

The righteous, who are genuinely puzzled, ask, "Lord, when did we see you hungry, thirsty, naked?" They are far past the point of toting up their good works. Because they are resting in the righteousness God has given them, they simply *do* because their hearts move them to do it. They don't even know to whom they're ministering. It doesn't matter.

A further paradox: Those who are secure in their God-given identities, experiencing the mystical union with Christ that Paul wrote about (Christ in me), are not even conscious of that reality. Keith Miller describes such a person:

> Although he may now be free to actualize that unique potential God has given him, his hope is that he will become more like Christ as he matures. And a strange thing seems to emerge—the more of his life he commits to God, the more creative and unique he may appear to be to others. People feel the Christ-like love of God coming through such a person, but he doesn't feel "like Jesus." He feels and looks free and interested in others.
>
> At a conference for ministers several years ago we were talking about Christian loving concern. One young man said, "I wonder how it would feel to love people the way Jesus did?" A silence followed. Then a white-haired minister said thoughtfully, "A Christian would probably never know. If you were loving people the way Jesus did, you'd be concentrating totally on the other person and his problems . . . and not on how you were feeling."[1]

LAMPS, SPICE, AND PERFUME

Nietzsche once wrote of the followers of Jesus Christ: They "will have to look more saved if I am to believe in their savior." Jesus in His Sermon on the Mount called for us to live in the fullness of His grace for the sake of such observers, watching from the world's darkness. "You are the light of the world," He proclaimed. "Let your light so shine before men, that they may see your good works and give glory to your Father who is in heaven" (Matthew 5:14, 16). How illogical it would be for someone to light a lamp and then put it under a basket! It is intended, He said, to give light "to all in the house" (Matthew 5:15).

This metaphor may be seen as a picture of us as individual believers set in our own spheres of influence, our "houses." God has lit each one of us with the particular "wattage" He desires, and He has placed us in a particular spot. In that place, if we burn clean and bright with His indwelling Spirit, we can be used to enlighten those around us with the evidence of Jesus' Lordship in this world.

Jesus also said of His disciples: "You are the salt of the earth." Many interpretations have been offered for this metaphor, but here are the main ideas. Like salt, which by its essence preserves meat from spoiling, we, by the purity and honesty of God's heart within us, can help preserve the world from its inherent evil and decay. As salt is a cleansing element, so, too, we, even as we uphold God's standards of righteousness and morality, can at the same time be agents of forgiveness and mercy. And as salt is a relish, we can bring life, hope, and joy into situations that are bleak with tedium or discouragement.

It has also been pointed out that salt creates thirst. Part of our function in the world is to cause others to hunger and thirst for the righteousness and the wholeness they see in our lives. Paul confided that he deliberately magnified his ministry to the Gentiles "in order to make my fellow Jews jealous" (Romans 11:14). C. J. Mahaney, a minister in the Washington, D.C., area, says, "I want everyone who hears me preach to go away dying of thirst for my Lord and for the living water that only He can give."

Yet another metaphor likens believers to irresistible perfume. Using the picture of triumphal parades of the conquering Roman soldiers so familiar to his original readers, Paul writes in 2 Corinthians 2:14–16:

> But thanks be to God, who in Christ always leads us in triumph, and through us spreads the fragrance of the knowledge of him everywhere. For we are the aroma of Christ to God among those who are being saved and among those who are perishing; to one a fragrance from death to death, to the other a fragrance from life to life.

To God we are a beautiful fragrance, for we remind Him of His beloved Son. To those who are being drawn to God our imputed sweetness acts like the fragrance of flowers to honeybees. (Only to those who are hardening their hearts, resisting the Holy Spirit's hand upon them, do we signal doom, just as the smell of garlands and incense of a victory parade meant humiliation and death to the defeated army.)

In short, we are "Christophers"—"Christ-bearers"—into whatever part of the world God has sent us. To the degree we are whole and transparent, to that extent we will show forth Him whom they have been yearning for (without even knowing it), the "desire of the nations" (Haggai 2:7).

Most followers of Jesus Christ, as John Howe has pointed out, can trace their progress toward wholeness in the Lord by the "great cloud of witnesses" He has put in our paths. These are the souls, living and dead, whom we've known or read or read about, who at a particular season or place in our journeys have incarnated some aspect of the Lord that we needed to see and experience. In my own life I am indebted to scores of such Christ-bearers, but there are, of course, major "landmarks"—people who have embodied certain qualities to me. From my own father's character I learned about the Father of mercies: His approachability, His eagerness to listen, His ready forgiveness, and His refusal to hold grudges. In my mother's deep walk with the Lord I witnessed Jesus the Intercessor: His sacrificial love, His compassion, His self-discipline, the power and the costliness of His prayers. In my relationship with my husband, Michael, I first experienced and have continued to be healed by Jesus Christ the Servant, by the power of His unconditional love, His unfailing dependability, His thorough and quiet service and His unembellished honesty. In my friend and teacher Barbara Twork I first saw Jesus the Teacher and learned how He delights in His Word, His sweetness, the personal quality of His knowledge of us and our special needs and desires, and His sense of humor. These were the "lights" in my house, through whom the Word became flesh, drawing me and teaching me until I could recognize Him for myself.

Today, as I look around at my sisters and brothers in the Lord I marvel at the light, salt, and fragrance He spreads through them. Through Bruce and Casey He brings standards of excellence (and healing laughter) into the midst of an ambitious and sophisticated design team in a giant corporation. Through Margie and Delphine and Larry and Ruth He listens and gives wise and loving counsel to men, women, and children who are weary and in need of being really "heard." Through Mary, Suzanne, Evans, and Lois He shows the world His touches of beauty through art and song and dance. Through Michael and Scott and Bill He establishes oases of sanity and truth in the wilderness of bureaucracy, business, and high-tech industry. Through Ron and Bill and Sue He ministers healing, from a home clinic serving tiny Oklahoma towns to the operating rooms of a metropolitan hospital. Through Christy and Beth and Laura and Deborah He fights for the right of the unborn to experience His love. Through Wil and Helene He proclaims His truth in the skeptical realms of science and politics. Through Josie and Peggy He loves and serves children who might never know affirming love at all. Through Mark and Mike and Barbara and Sarah He shows the riches of His Word to all who will hear it. My brothers and sisters are in the world, but they are not of it, for their true home is in the Light Itself, and in their good works they give Him the praise.

What salt He scatters! What a fragrance He spreads in the lives of these individuals as they "live, and move, and have their being" in Him.

A CITY SET ON A HILL

Thomas Smail in *Reflected Glory* likens individual Christians to a circle of mirrors set around the Lord:

Each has its own glint of brightness, the reflection that is appropriate from that angle and in that situation, but it takes all the mirrors in right relationship to one another to reflect that brightness of the light from every angle. So the complete glory of Christ can be exhibited only in the complete Body of His people, as the Spirit reflects Him, personally but not privately in the life that they share. The adequate mirror of Christ's glory can only be the whole Church of God.[2]

As influential and powerful as we can be as single lamps, the real power comes in a collection of lights: "A city set on a hill," the Lord Jesus declared, "*cannot* be hid." When single lights come together, we are like a city situated on a point so high that nothing can obscure its visibility—not even the miasma of the world's darkness.

Through the prophet Isaiah, God speaks of the glorious day when Jerusalem, His people, will come into their collective identity and will draw the world like a magnet by the beauty of its holiness. We can almost hear the joy in His voice as He calls to them:

Arise, shine; for your light has come, and the glory of the Lord has risen upon you. For behold, darkness shall cover the earth, and thick darkness the peoples; but the Lord will arise upon you, and his glory will be seen upon you. And nations shall come to your light, and kings to the brightness of your rising.   Isaiah 60:1–3

What will be the nature of this light that shines from His people, drawing all the nations and even their rulers to the truth? What will unbelievers see in God's Church that will cause them to come "streaming" to it? If we, each one, are living in the fullness of what God has created us to be, what the world will see is God's supernatural love, His real and unlimited power, and His unfathomable hope.

SUPERNATURAL LOVE

On His last night with them, Jesus said to His disciples:

A new commandment I give to you, that you love one another; even as I have loved you, that you also love one another. By this all men

*will know that you are my disciples, if you have love for one
another.*   John 13:34–35

Why did Jesus call this a "new" commandment? From the very
beginning God had summed up the Law by saying we were to
love Him "with all our hearts, souls, minds and strength," and
that we were to "love our neighbors as ourselves." Love had
been the constant theme of all Jesus' teaching, the hallmark of
all His activity. What here is "new"?

"Even as I have loved you" is the new element. No longer
were they required merely to love their neighbor. No more
was it sufficient to surpass the Pharisee's righteousness by
showing charity to enemies. No longer was the Law—do
unto others as you would have them do unto you—sufficient
criterion. For Jesus' disciples, for those to whom He was
entrusting the proclamation of the Gospel to the world, the
whole concept of love was being stretched beyond all human
standards. Jesus was commanding them to love each other *as
He had loved them*, with total compassion, with total concentration, with total forgiveness, with divine *agape* love, the
kind that would sacrifice its own welfare without a second of
hesitation, that would lay down its life for a friend. Totally,
unequivocally, and to the death.

Kenneth Wuest's expanded translation of the New Testament gives an especially vivid expression to the kind of love
Jesus was commissioning, as Peter understood it:

> . . . *Having purified your souls by means of your obedience to the
> truth, resulting in not an assumed but a genuine affection and
> fondness for the brethren, an affection and fondness that springs from
> your hearts by reason of the pleasure you take in them; from the heart
> love each other with an intense reciprocal love that springs from your
> hearts because of your estimation of the preciousness of the brethren,
> and which is divinely self-sacrificial in its essence, having been
> begotten again not of perishable seed but of imperishable, through the
> word of God which lives and abides.*   1 Peter 1:22–23

If we were to love each other in this way, Jesus said, all men would know that we are His disciples. How? If we are all being ourselves, there will be great diversity. But if we are all being ourselves, in obedience to Jesus, there will also be great harmony, just as all the varied instruments of an orchestra can be combined into a symphony, though they are individually quite different. In the world, harmony can only be produced by imposing uniformity, a process that results in superficial or temporary harmony at best. Therefore, if the world should ever see Jew and Gentile, male and female, black and white united in genuine love, organically knit together, taking pleasure in each other and estimating each other as "precious," they will know that they are witnessing something not of this world. They they will begin to believe that Jesus does indeed live.

Such love caused the world to take notice, even in Christianity's infancy. In a report to the emperor Hadrian (c. 124 A.D.), a man named Aristides commented:

> They love one another. They never fail to help widows; they save orphans from those who would hurt them. If they have something, they give freely to the man who has nothing; if they see a stranger, they take him home, and are happy, as though he were a real brother. They don't consider themselves brothers in the usual sense, but brothers instead, through the spirit, in God.

SUPERNATURAL POWER

If we are being our true selves, we will be functioning in the exact places and ways God has designed. If in the Body of Christ the ears are being ears, the hands are being hands, and each is answering to the Head, the Lord Jesus Christ, then the world will see His power unleashed once more. Jesus said, "Greater works than these shall you do" (John 14:12). In His incarnation Jesus' power was limited somewhat by time and space and the finitude of a human body. A host of believers, filled with His Spirit and obedient to His call upon them, could surpass His earthly capacity to heal, teach, and deliver.

But this power will only be realized if all parts are functioning in concert. Everett (Terry) Fullam, Episcopal priest and Bible teacher, draws a grotesque picture of the Body composed of people who are not submitted to Jesus' Lordship. If each believer is inventing himself according to his own ideas of Christianity, or cloning himself to a Christian "celebrity" or clinging to old denominational identities, the result is "a Frankenstein, a great spastic monster," stumbling ineffectually through the world, like the Pharisees offending and frightening away the true seekers, those "who would see Jesus" (John 12:20). Moving in concert, of one mind and heart, united in love, agreeing in prayer, each one striving for maturity as the person God has created him or her to be, the Body of Christ will be revealed in power and truth and a glory so bright it cannot be refuted or ignored.

A HOPE AND A WELCOME

Finally, in our redemption, the world will see a hope for itself.

Somehow, if we are living as Jesus Christ directs us, if we are answering to His voice as He calls us by our new names, the world will see in us not *our* perfection, but His. We shall be whole, and yet that wholeness will not obscure its Source. Even as we recognize that the scarlets, purples, and blues of a stained-glass window only come into their deepest and most vivid trueness when the light pours through them, so the world will see that the reason for our beauty is the true Light of the World who permeates our beings. In our imputed splendor they will receive hope, if we proclaim the Gospel in its purity and humbly give the glory to our Redeemer. When He interjected Himself into human history, the Lord of the Universe chose for Himself a human lineage marked by peasants, harlots, Gentiles, tyrants, and foreigners as well as shepherds and kings. When the world can see that He has deigned to come in and dwell in a spectrum of humanity just as wide, they might begin to believe His invitation: *"Whosoever will* may come."

THE REWARDED NAME

In C. S. Lewis' masterpiece *The Great Divorce*, he writes of heaven as a place where, at long last, reality is revealed, as a place where we no longer have to strain to see, "as through a glass darkly" (1 Corinthians 13:12), but where things are shown to be what they truly are, stripped of all earthly pretense. In Lewis' heaven, the tables are turned: "Heavy-weight" theologians are revealed as puny, nattering ghosts with "unsubstantial lips," while anonymous, kind little housewives become great queens, with faces of "unbearable beauty." The character, the name of each, known during earthly life only to God, is now made manifest before all creation.

In one sense, we shall not receive our full names until we are face to face with the One who has created and recreated us upon this earth. Our "soul's picture," as George MacDonald has called the new name, is

> what God thinks about the man. . . . It is the divine judgment, . . . the "Come, thou blessed," spoken to the individual.
>
> It is only when the man has become his name that God gives him the stone with the name upon it, for then first can he understand what his name signifies. It is the blossom, the perfection, the completeness, that determines the name: and God foresees that from the first because He made it so: but the tree of the soul, before its blossom comes, cannot understand what blossom it is to bear and could not know what the word meant. . . . To tell the name is to seal the success—to say "In thee also I am well pleased."[3]

As we await the coming of that day of the Lord when we as individuals or as a Church meet Him who brought us out of Idea and into Reality, we can hold fast to yet another promise. To those who have received the vision of their new identities, who have cherished their new names and have striven to yield to the hand of the Divine Potter, an eternal name awaits, the most precious of all. Jesus promises our reward:

> *He who conquers, I will make him a pillar in the temple of my God; never shall he go out of it, and I will write on him the name of my God, and the name of the city of my God, the new Jerusalem which comes down from my God out of heaven, and my own new name.*
>
> Revelation 3:12

God's own name, His holy and eternal identity, shall be forever a part of our own.

Love is calling us by name. Lord Jesus Christ, give us the ears to hear and the courage to answer.

NOTES

Chapter 1
1 Michael Esses, *Jesus in Genesis* (Plainfield, N.J.: Logos International, 1974), p. 64.
2 Arthur W. Pink, *Gleanings in Genesis* (Chicago: Moody Press, 1922), p. 289.
3 Pink, p. 292.

Chapter 2
1 Manford George Gutzke, *Plain Talk on John* (Grand Rapids, Mich.: Zondervan Publishing House, 1968), p. 21.
2 F. B. Meyer, *Peter: Fisherman, Disciple, Apostle* (New York: Fleming H. Revell, 1920), p. 7.
3 Herbert Lockyer, *All the Apostles of the Bible* (Grand Rapids, Mich.: Zondervan Publishing House, 1972), p. 209.
4 *The Interpreter's Bible*, Vol. IX (New York: Abingdon Press, 1954), p. 170.
5 William Barclay, *The Acts of the Apostles* (Philadelphia: The Westminster Press, 1953), p. 64.
6 *The Interpreter's Bible*, p. 170.

Chapter 3
1 Nathan J. Stone, *Names of God in the Old Testament* (Chicago: Moody Press, 1944), pp. 11–12.
2 Alfred Marshall, *The Revised Standard Version Interlinear Greek-English New Testament* (Grand Rapids, Mich.: Zondervan Publishing House, 1958), p. 465.
3 William Barclay, *New Testament Words* (Philadelphia: The Westminster Press, 1974), p. 280.

Chapter 4
1 Paul Brand and Philip Yancey, *Fearfully and Wonderfully Made* (Grand Rapids, Mich.: Zondervan Publishing House, 1980), pp. 46–47.
2 Thomas Merton, *Contemplative Prayer* (Garden City, N.Y.: Image Books, 1969), p. 69.
3 Thomas A. Smail, *Reflected Glory: The Spirit in Christ and Christians* (Grand Rapids, Mich.: William B. Eerdman's Publishing Co., 1975), pp. 25–26.
4 F. B. Meyer, *Great Verses Through the Bible* (Grand Rapids, Mich.: Zondervan Publishing House, 1972), p. 427.

Chapter 5
1 *Interpreter's Bible*, Vol. XII (New York: Abingdon Press, 1954), pp. 386–387.
2 Jackie Pullinger, *Chasing the Dragon* (London: Hodder & Stoughton, 1980), pp. 23–28.
3 Corrie ten Boom with John and Elizabeth Sherrill, *The Hiding Place* (New York: Bantam Books, Inc., 1974), pp. 235–236.

4 Malcolm Muggeridge, *Something Beautiful for God: Mother Teresa of Calcutta* (Garden City, N.Y.: Image Press, 1977), p. 16.
5 Paul Brand and Philip Yancey, *Fearfully and Wonderfully Made* (Grand Rapids, Mich.: Zondervan Publishing House, 1980), p. 198.
6 Elisabeth Elliot, *Through Gates of Splendor* (Wheaton, Ill.: Tyndale House Publishers, Inc., 1956), pp. 13–14.
7 J. I. Packer, *Keep in Step with the Spirit* (Old Tappan, N.J.: Fleming H. Revell Co., 1984).
8 C. S. Lewis, ed., *George MacDonald: An Anthology* (New York: Macmillan Publishing Company, 1947), p. 9.

Chapter 6
1 John and Paula Sandford, *The Transformation of the Inner Man* (Plainfield, N.J.: Bridge Publishing, Inc., 1982), pp. 41–42.
2 Kenneth S. Wuest, *The New Testament: An Expanded Translation* (Grand Rapids, Mich.: William B. Eerdman's Publishing Co., 1961), p. 373.
3 Oswald Chambers, *My Utmost for His Highest* (New York: Dodd, Mead & Co., 1935), p. 28.

Chapter 7
1 This story is taken from a taped testimony given by Jill Briscoe and is recounted in her book, *There's a Snake in My Garden* (Grand Rapids, Mich.: Zondervan Publishing House, 1975).
2 Jamie Buckingham, *Risky Living: Keys to Inner Healing* (Plainfield, N.J.: Logos International, 1976), pp. 94–95.
3 Paul Tournier, *The Meaning of Persons* (New York: Harper & Row, Publishers Inc., 1957), pp. 171.
4 Tournier, pp. 191–192.

Chapter 8
1 C. S. Lewis, ed., *George MacDonald, An Anthology* (New York: Macmillan Publishing Company, 1947), p. 56.
2 Edward B. Pusey, trans., *The Confessions of St. Augustine* (New York: Collier Books, 1961), p. 131.
3 John and Paula Sandford, *The Transformation of the Inner Man* (Plainfield, N.J.: Bridge Publishing, Inc., 1982), pp. 10–11.
4 Paul Tournier, *The Meaning of Persons* (New York: Harper & Row, Publishers Inc., 1957), p. 210.
5 C. S. Lewis, *Mere Christianity* (New York: Macmillan Publishing Co., 1964).
6 Karen Burton Mains, *Open Heart—Open Home* (Elgin, Ill.: David C. Cook Publishing Co., 1976), pp. 119–120.

Chapter 9
1 Keith Miller, *The Becomers* (Waco, Tex.: Word Books, 1973), p. 136.
2 Thomas A. Smail, *Reflected Glory: The Spirit in Christ and Christians* (Grand Rapids, Mich.: Zondervan Publishing House, 1975), pp. 28–29.
3 C. S. Lewis, ed., *George MacDonald: An Anthology* (New York: Macmillan Publishing Company, 1947), pp. 7–8.